DIARY

OF A

FIRST-GENERATION

COLLEGE STUDENT

PART I: STORIES & STEPS TOWARD YOUR COLLEGE SUCCESS

By Antonio Miranda

For Inquiries Contact:

https://www.antonionutrition.com/contact

Alternatively, scan the QR code below:

Acknowledgements

Thank you to the following individuals for their skilled contributions to the creation of this book. Adrian Gazaway as primary editor. Jeston Texeira as formatter. Jacy Joplin as graphic designer. AS, BS, JF, JGL, and JKLM as beta readers. Together, we made this book possible.

Book Guide

This book is available in paperback, E-book, and audio.

Paperback and E-book: Available on Amazon

Audio: This version provides a narration of each chapter through the reading of the author plus bonus content.

For links to each of these options, please visit:

https://www.antonionutrition.com/

Alternatively, scan the QR code below:

To contact the author or request a speaking or business inquiry please visit:

https://www.antonionutrition.com/contact

Alternatively, scan the QR code below:

DISCLAIMER

The content of this book is for educational purposes. The stories and concepts in this book are not financial nor official lifestyle advice. The guidance provided is circumstantial and best used to psychologically ease the burden of college. No formal relationship between the author and reader is formed. It is the responsibility of the reader to seek proper assistance through the various resources provided on their college campus.

The author is not to be held accountable for changes in the political or philosophical perspectives of anyone quoted or referenced in this book. Many chapters highlight quotes and stories from famous individuals. Given the nature of the world today, the public and legal stance on these individuals may change. It is not the responsibility of the author to adapt this publication in response to these social and legal changes. Every quote and story serve to provide information to the reader on a particular subject. The quote or story should be seen independently within the context of the book. Inclusion of these individuals does not equate to endorsement of their beliefs in this ever changing political and philosophical world.

The author acknowledges his lens as a Christian, Mexican American, first-generation college student. My experience is not representative of all first-generation students. I choose to share my cultural and religious background, however, to encourage understanding of all cultures and creeds. We can learn from everyone, no matter their background.

PROLOGUE

As a first-generation college student, I was the first to do many things. I was the first in my family to move away from home to attend university, the first to experience the culture shock of college and of a random roommate, the first to nearly fail two classes and not have anyone to call, and the first to face the fear of letting my family down in the face of such academic opportunity.

Being the first was tough in so many ways, but oh so beautiful in others. I was the first to travel abroad, the first to experience the joy of coming home for the holidays and have everyone admire and encourage me, the first to overcome academic failure, and the first to cross that beautiful commencement stage not once, not twice, but three times (BS, MS, and PhD).

If you ask me what helped me survive ten years of school, the simple answer would be an attitude of determination and gratitude. From the very beginning and through the highs and lows of my ten year journey I was always determined to make my family and my future self proud. I wanted to honor the sacrifice of everyone that came before me: my siblings, parents, grandparents, and beyond. I was determined to carry the torch as each generation is called to do. We're all first gens in something, so I saw it as an honor and a beautiful cross to bear. Being the first is a part of life, and I was always grateful to be the one to do it first. I was, and forever will be, a first-generation college student. What an honor it was and still is. Thank God.

CONTENTS

PREFACE

A bit of context about me, the author, before you proceed to learn about college through the lens of my experience. My lens is one of a workaholic. I loved to study and work hard, but, as you will read, often in excess. Therefore, much of the book encourages you to slow down and balance school and fun. If you, however, find yourself having "too much" fun, then be wise and don't use this book as an excuse to party too hard.

Another lens of mine, for better or worse, is describing my studies and career almost as a "debt to pay" to the hardworking generation that laid the path for our generation. As I write in the book, however, viewing hard work as a "debt to pay" is an incorrect view on life. College is an opportunity to honor your past, while also honoring your own future. No matter your past, parents, or mentors, the journey is now yours to forge. Do it for whomever you'd like, but don't forget to do it for your future self.

Additionally, I hope you are able to read in between the lines and see that I love to learn. I loved what I studied and will forever love learning about anything. If you are not as passionate about learning as I am, know that is okay. I fell in love with academic learning, but not everyone is meant to love academics. College is the time to figure out whether you love a particular study, should focus on a trade, or should find a manageable profession where you can still have time to love other areas beyond your career. Take what helps. Leave what does not. God bless your journey.

Important: Before You Start College

As I approached my senior year in high school, I remember not putting much thought into my future. I was in my routine of school, sports, and friends. I wasn't stressed about college or my career because 1) I had chosen to not participate in an early college program (because I was focused on sports and grades to a fault), 2) I was a bit lazy to do anything outside of my routine, and 3) in part because I was a first-generation student without much of a roadmap or a game plan. I was a hard worker, but a poor planner!

Then, one day at the end of my junior year in high school, I remember saying goodbye to one of my senior friends. He was planning to attend the University of Arkansas in the fall. As we said our goodbyes, he looked at me with a smile and asked "where do you plan on going next year, man?" That's when it hit me: I had literally no idea. I had yet to think about, even less plan, what I wanted to do after high school.

A few months later, my senior year English teacher paused mid-lecture and shared words of wisdom that I never forgot. "Have you all considered that a year from now (the start of freshman year of college) your life will be completely different? A new place, new people..." I don't remember what else she said, but it made all of us seniors pause (especially me: a laid-back procrastinator of the top 10% in my class). For the first time college was not a distant event. The time to start planning for college was now.

In retrospect, my English teacher was 100% right. Senior year flies by and life quickly changes soon after you graduate. The end of grade school marks the end of your life as you know it. The routine, responsibility, and consequences of life shift from your parents and your teachers, to... you. You've probably heard this from your parents and mentors, so I won't repeat what you already know. They are right by the way, on making your bed, getting up on time, not missing assignments or class, etc.... so take them seriously.

If you won't listen to your parents or mentors, at least listen to a guy (me) that was once in your shoes. Stop waiting for someone else to initiate the college talk. Start thinking and planning for YOUR future. Your senior year comes and goes quickly. Whether you're scared, excited, or anything in between, the time to talk and plan for college is now.

Before you start college, you need to ask yourself a few questions. Otherwise, you might find yourself years behind, bored out of your mind, or in massive debt from going or avoiding college. Take a moment to get off your phone and write out your responses and ideas to these questions:

What do I want to be when I grow up?

This is a question everyone asks themselves repeatedly from childhood and well into adulthood (just ask your parents or mentors; nobody ever has life fully figured out). So, if you're not 100% sure of your career goal, that's okay. It's actually normal to be unsure. Meet with your college/career counselor, go online, and look up potential careers and salaries.

Find what sparks your will to learn and make a difference in the world (be it plumbing or business). Or, at the very least, find what keeps you busy, making money, and out of trouble. As the saying goes, the devil makes use of idle hands. Thankfully, the opposite is also true: "the plans of the diligent lead surely to abundance." Plan ahead, work hard, and your life will be better. For more on choosing a personally and financially fulfilling career, see chapter 2.

Your Response/Thoughts to the Question Here:

_____

_____

_____

_____

_____

Do I need to go to college to achieve my career goal?

Many college books won't tell you this: college is not for everyone. You do not have to go to college to be "successful." There are many entrepreneurial and manual labor jobs that may or may not benefit from a degree. These careers provide great opportunities without having to go into college debt. You might aspire to start a successful lawn mowing business or a creative online store. No matter what you choose, make sure you determine the value of a career to your life and the value of a degree to your career. Go talk to your college counselor.

That being said, don't skip college because you are lazy or stubborn. Don't blow off college simply because your parents and teachers pestered you about it for months. Don't skip college because a one in a million guy became a billionaire from his parents' basement. Don't skip college just to be different.

Not going to college is not about avoiding responsibility. It's about opportunity relative to your career goals. I promise, if you avoid college because of pride, fear, or laziness, you will end up way worse than your friends who do go to college. Not because you didn't get a diploma, but because you let pride, fear, or laziness become a norm in your life.

The good news is, you're still young enough to figure things out. If you are unsure of what you want to do, then try work that interests you and some community college classes. Eventually, by learning what you dread and what you dream of, you will figure out where your purpose lies. College or not, choose to challenge yourself; it's the best thing to do with your time! See chapter 9 for tips from previous college graduates on starting college. Keep it simple: combine your talents, passion, and something that makes enough money/people pay for.

In summary, before you learn to master college, you need to find out if college is even right for you. Don't go to college because everyone else is doing it. Have intent. Make a plan. Don't be afraid to take the less traveled path of early college classes, a gap year, entrepreneurship, or manual labor. The most important thing is that you learn to make a living: financially, morally, socially, and beyond. Learn to ask the right questions, meet the right people, plan ahead, and to embrace the learning of life.

In my case, I did exactly what I encourage you not to do (that's why I wrote this book)! I applied to college because it's what my friends did, and I procrastinated and waited until the last minute to apply. I didn't know the value of a dollar, nor how to balance my budget. I pursued a major without looking into future finances or career potential. I simply followed the general plan: finish high school, go to college for "my passion," and wish for the best.

The good news is, even with all my mistakes, I still made it work. I was in college for 10 years and obtained three degrees while working part or full time throughout. I had a blast, worked hard, and learned a ton. I figured out my talents and passion, and turned them into a financially feasible and fun purpose in life. Whatever your college journey (be it 0 or 14 years) with the proper guidance, imagine what you can do. Do better than I did. The real learning of life starts now!

CHAPTER 1: WELCOME TO COLLEGE

How to Handle the College Transition as a First-Generation Pioneer

"Change the way you look at things and the things you look at change." –Wayne W. Dyer

When I started college, I was a confident but unknowingly clueless freshman student. My dream was simple: pursue my passion and make my immigrant parents proud. I was in school for a decade, from August 2012 to August 2022. Yes, you read that right: ten years.

I'm a first-generation college student turned PhD. Like my parents, however, my knowledge did not come from my diplomas. Though my parents never stepped foot in a college classroom, they earned their PhD in life. Likewise, over the course of ten years I earned my PhD in nutrition, but simultaneously my PhD in life as a first-generation college student. In my success I gained humility. In my suffering I gained wisdom. These are my stories. Take from them what you can. They will likely be your stories too. From first-generation college student to whatever you choose to be. Sí se puede, sí se pudo, y siempre se va a poder (Yes we can. Yes we will and yes we will always be able to [achieve our goals].

Welcome to College

Starting college is one of the weirdest, most challenging times in your life. It's a time where every student will face two major struggles: 1) change, and 2) pressure. First, change: change in your surroundings, friends, family, and even change in yourself. Second, pressure: pressure to find friends, ace your classes, make your family proud, avoid the "freshman 15" (the common weight gain from life stress upon starting college), get enough sleep, and to "find yourself" (whatever that means). While the changes and pressures of college may seem overwhelming, don't let them be. College is the start of an amazing adventure! It's your time to not only live to learn, but learn to live. Welcome to college!

1) The "C" in College is for "Change"

College is a "culture shock". This is the phrase you will hear tossed around throughout your freshman year, but what does that even mean? It means that most students are surprised or even uncomfortable ("shocked") in their new home (college). The changes in place, people, politics, and much more can leave you feeling isolated or even alienated ("like I don't fit in").

You might not notice it, but the culture shock of college comes in a series of waves. First, you might feel uncomfortable as you start the first day of your college orientation surrounded by other awkward, shy, or "try hard to fit in" freshmen. The new school colors, and cheers will seem foreign and feel weird to chant. Even partaking in hallmark traditions of your university might at first seem weird and borderline bizarre. "Am I a bad student for not loving the traditions yet? Should I even go here?" Deep breath: you are normal!

The next "culture shock wave" of college comes from being dropped off by your family on move in day (or arriving on your own)! You might feel excited, but also unsure. This is the first time in your life that you will be on your own. Your dad will carry up the last item up to your dorm: the heavy TV. In the background your mom cries as she prepares to say goodbye. You might share a final meal together before they hit the road. You hug your family goodbye and fake a smile to reassure them that you're going to be okay. The reality is, things will never be the same, but you are still too naive to know it. Then they drive away and you break down in tears of sadness or tears of excitement because... freedom! Deep breath: no matter your reaction, you are normal.

Next comes the culture shock wave of making new friends. College may be the first time you have to actively "work" to make and sustain friendships. You might feel lost as you struggle to make friends or if your college friend group seems completely different from high school. You might have a random roommate with different beliefs and behaviors compared to yours! Whether it takes you one day, one week, or one year to find friends, this is normal!

Next comes the culture shock wave of starting classes. Your first day will likely involve a lecture hall full of excited freshmen. The professor will seem cool because they cuss during lecture, but also seem scary because of the workload. After class the students will line the doorway to shake the professor's hand, because well "everyone said it's a good idea to meet the professor." FYI: your professor will remember you more if you go to office hours (located in the syllabus, this is the designated time outside of class when the professor is available in their office for students to visit and ask questions) vs if you try to meet them on day one amid the line of 300 other freshman faces.

Amid these changes in place, people, politics, and perspectives comes the most challenging change of all: the reality that YOU will change. Your mind will hold on to your old identity as it tries to adapt to a new environment. Change will seem uncomfortable as your mind tries to balance "who I was before college" and "who I want to be."

Your "senioritis" (the laziness during the last year of high school) will be abruptly replaced by long nights of studying. Surviving your freshman "weed-out" classes (1st and 2nd year courses that are typically difficult so that only the high-performing students can progress further. These are most common in science, technology, engineering, and math programs, but also business and pre-med) will mean an endless to-do list.

Conversely, college stress and freedom lead some into habits of excessive partying and skipping classes (a slippery slope, so... be careful)! You might even find yourself gravitating more toward or drifting away from your lifelong religion. No matter the choices you make, the newfound college freedom will change you.

Along with these college changes, comes the journey of a lifetime: finding which changes work for you. How much studying can you handle without mentally ruining yourself? How much fun can you have, while still achieving your academic goals? How often should you go or call home? How do you make genuine friends? What career is right for me? How do I become a better person that I, my parents, and my higher power can be proud of? What parts of my former self were an "act" to fit in and WHO AM I?

These questions might sound like an ice breaker to your freshman philosophy class. However, they are all questions you will live through as you try to find balance amid the college chaos. Many say the "C" in college stands for change. Now you know why.

How do I know so much about the college culture shock? Because I and my classmates, like all first-generation college students (first gens), lived it too. Each of the above stories is based on my own struggles from freshman year. Wave after wave, every student will experience college in their own unique way.

I share these first-gen phenomena so you know that you are not alone. Struggling with culture shock, making friends, wrestling with your identity, and surviving classes; everyone goes through it. The reality is, all of the concerns and challenges you will face have been overcome by thousands of students before you. Decades of first-gen students precede you and have felt the same pressure and college nerves. Similarly, right now there are thousands of other first-gens facing the same challenges you face. So before you start overthinking college, stop. Take a deep breath. You're amazing, and you're going to do amazing things no matter the challenges and changes. Change is your secret ingredient to success.

2) Pressure as a First-Generation Student

As the first in our family to go to college, first-generation students face constant unfamiliarities. We are the first to experience the college application process, moving to a new place, unforgiving professors, endless studying, sleepless nights, and so much more. At times it seems like everyone else around you "has it figured out." Students will say "I'm a 3rd generation student of this university" or "I knew I would go here since I was 8 years old."

Meanwhile your parents didn't go to college. Your family has no "university legacy." You're at the university because it made financial sense (hopefully)! You find yourself studying constantly because you have no family finances to fall back on. In our mind, the mind of a first gen, it's now or never. For us, college is a sacrifice not just for me, but for my family. For us, college is the way we honor the sacrifice of our parents and those who came before us. Yes, we view college as great fun and the time of our life. This fun, however, is overshadowed by the need to "survive" and "set the bar high" for our family.

Given our circumstances, the overarching challenge we all face as first-gens is summarized in one word: pressure. This pressure comes from both internal and external avenues. Intrinsically we feel pressure from our own academic standards and career goals ("how could I let myself get a C when I am an A student? I'm never getting into medical school!"). We then internalize this pressure because no one else in our family can relate to these inescapable stressors.

As first-gens we also feel pressure from carrying the burden of expectation from our family. In our pursuit to "carry the torch" for our family, we place immense pressure on our shoulders. This pressure is only made worse when you return home after a difficult semester. Your mom introduces you as the "the future doctor of the family" (because they innocently mistake any healthcare degree with an MD). Next your aunts and uncles begin to ask you random medical and personal health questions. All the while you feel overwhelmed and think "I'm no doctor. I can't even get an A in chemistry."

Conversely, many first gens start college with unsupportive families and friends groups. You call home to celebrate a high grade, only to be shown deflating indifference. You call your friends for emotional support, but they don't understand and may even shame you. Despite your motivation, you feel alone. This is the pressure of a first-generation college student.

College: Asking for Help While Remaining Independent

What, then, is the solution to handling the changes and pressures of college? How can you succeed as a pioneer in a new land (university) with a long road ahead of you? The answer is simple: remember that pioneers go farther together! To keep it real: you need to learn to seek help!

- Make friends with other supportive first-generation students.
- Stay involved in freshman-success organizations.
- Find upperclassmen mentors in your department.
- Join organizations that align with your career goals.
- At the bare minimum, watch YouTube videos for support!
- Learn to be resourceful and ask for HELP!

Take advantage of the free resources provided by your university. You will find student counseling services, help lines, financial aid, scholarship opportunities, career counselors, food pantries, and so much more. Given this information, know that the university wants you to succeed. The help is there on every college campus. Seek and you shall find. While I'm sure you are awesome and smart, stop relying exclusively on yourself. Ask for help.

Lastly, as you begin your college journey remember that help will come to you in unexpected forms, if you are open to seek it. Lean on your resources, your friends, and yes, your family. Remember that your parents, no matter their background, were once pioneers. As first-generation college students we are privileged to have role models who are immigrants or low-income, masters of resourcefulness and resolve. Lean on them for advice and inspiration from their life experience. Because, though your parents will never pass an SAT, trust me, they are some of the smartest people you will ever know.

Conversely, in the case you do not have a supportive family: 1) stay in touch with your high school mentors or seek out mentors at the university, or 2) give your family [in some cases] another chance. You might be surprised at how supportive some members of your family can be… if you let your walls down. Being vulnerable is scary and risky, but it's worth finding that person that will always be in your corner to support you.

You were bred from pioneers: thus, you are a pioneer. You have it in you to be independent, resourceful, and unwavering. Don't forget to work hard, have fun, and make life better by mastering when and how to ask for help. Your future is in your own hands. Welcome to college!

P.S.

Do not fall for the incorrect label of first-generation college students as "underserved and disadvantaged." This is simply not true. First gens often receive greater financial aid, scholarships, and academic support programs. First-gens, such as yourself, have unwavering grit, work ethic, and critical thinking skills beyond your imagination. Your upbringing, as hard as it may have been, has instilled these essential qualities in you without you knowing it.

When people ask me "what was your secret to college success?" I answer with, "being first generation: son of immigrant parents. Because they didn't have the opportunity for school, I love to learn. Because they worked so hard to make a living, I believe in myself to dream high on what I can achieve. Like my mom always says, *'sí se puede compadre'* (there's always a way, partner)."

What we lack in familial college experience, we can make up for in resources and perseverance. Never forget, a motivated first gen such as yourself equipped with the proper tools has the greatest advantages of all: drive and direction. As you will soon see, you are ready for college. Godspeed.

Chapter 1 Activity: Where to Find Help

Take 15 minutes to outline your support contact list. Take a picture/screenshot, then save it in a folder on your phone. This way, anytime you're in a panic and can't figure it out on your own, you'll know exactly where to go for help!

College Advice/Help

Dorm Resident Advisor:

Campus Counseling Services:

Trustworthy Family/Friend:

In an Emergency: *

Academic/Career Questions

Student Organizations:

My Advisor/Supplemental Advisor: **

Writing Center:

Professors/Tutoring:

Additional Important Information

Campus Health Services:

Campus Police/Security:

Auto/Car Help:

National Suicide and Crisis Lifeline: *Call/Text 988*

Yourself! Remember, college is about figuring out how to become independent (or at least... self-sufficient)!

*Know your apartment phone number, or reliable friend/family member.

**Some students are not very compatible with their "in-department" advisor. If this is the case for you, it might be worth meeting with an advisor in another department (such as one in a major you are considering changing to). Remember, your advisor is there to help you, but it's okay to ask for a second opinion.

CHAPTER 2: GOOGLE YOUR FUTURE SALARY

How to Choose a Career
You Won't Regret

(Disclaimer: This chapter is not financial advice!)

"Poor is not holy. Rich is not holy. Holy is holy...When you get some money: you serve the poor, you take care of people that are hurting, you lift people up, but you can't do that when you're broke." - Dave Ramsey

I'm going to be brutally honest because I care about you and your future. The BIGGEST mistakes I see among first gen students are always about money. As first gen students, our parents didn't go to college. This leads many of us to fall for the "higher education halo effect" (where we idolize anything university or degree related). As we prepare for college you hear "go to school so you don't have to work outdoors like me" from your uncle the roofer. Then your parents say, "I want you to get a diploma no matter the cost" (bad idea).

The reality is, our family never went to college, and there's no shame in that. Quite the opposite, I respect the heck out of anyone who works in the trades, manual labor, and entrepreneurship! While we all respect and love our parents, I'm here to tell you their ability to guide you in college and career decisions is very limited. If you are first gen, your parents won't be able to tell you how to choose a college that falls into your budget or a degree with a good return on investment. Worst of all, they won't have experience with the burden of student debt and how you should avoid/limit it as much as possible!

Who then can you turn to for college advice? Anyone with higher education experience that genuinely cares about your future. These include the career center, high school teachers, and many more (FYI: don't ask people in your college major's department. Their job is to help you graduate with the major you chose. Their job isn't to warn you about the potential financial limitations of your major).

That being said, don't underestimate your role in your future success. Ultimately, you get to choose and own the decisions in your life. Talk to people, watch videos, and think long and hard about what's best for you. Don't get sucked into "I just want to make my parents proud" like 99% of first gens (including myself). Instead think about "how do I make the FUTURE ME proud?" Future me (imagine yourself at 35 for example) will be proud of me for avoiding debt and choosing a major with opportunities. Future me will be proud of a high earning potential to avoid living paycheck to paycheck. Choosing to honor "FUTURE ME" is the best honor you could do for your family.

Don't just do college for your family. Do it for yourself. Do college in a way that, 10 years from now, sees you financially stable and at peace. That's when you'll truly make your family proud. When you're proud of yourself, both personally and financially. Seek guidance and ask yourself the HARD questions now. You'll thank me later.

Hard Money Questions

"How much money will I make if I pursue this major/degree path?" You MUST ask yourself this one question early in your college career (or ideally prior to high school graduation). While it might seem obvious, many first gens don't think to do this! Nor have you been told to research it (I know I didn't)! You MUST ask yourself money questions because no one else will. Knowing your journey toward financial prosperity or peril is the cornerstone of your future survival. Begin with the end in mind.

At this very moment do the following. Get on Google, type in "(insert your future job title) average salary." While you are at it, type in where you wish to live in the United States and type in "(insert your future job title) jobs near (insert future city/state where you wish to live) average salary." Though these salaries and job opportunities will vary due to regionality and change over time, the two questions provide a glimpse into your future. They will show you a) can you make enough money with your future career, and b) if you graduated today, where would you have to move to find that job.

Next, visit your university's career center. There you will find university-specific data on previous graduates in your major. You will be able to learn how grads performed in terms of employment and income. More specifically, there you will learn what percentage of graduates with your major found a job within 6 months after graduation, which area of the field they work in now, and how much they make. Reviewing this university-specific data will help you far beyond a Google search. Every university and degree are different. Learn to look ahead, so that you can make informed decisions. A degree is only as good as the opportunities it provides you.

I share this because when I was a freshman in university I was a part of an amazing program for first-generation college students called "FOCUS" (Foundation of Continued Undergraduate Success). We were all like you and your friends. We were all in our late teens, driven to make our family proud, and dedicated to our academic passion. One week, we participated in an activity where we estimated our expected monthly expenses after we graduated and were living on our own. This proved to be a difficult task for a group of naive and determined first-gens. Dedicated to our academic passions and career fantasies we twisted the reality of our future financial responsibilities. Rather than agreeing that certain career salaries make it nearly impossible to survive on your own (yes you read that correctly), we chose to live in ignorant bliss.

One student stood up and calculated that her expected 40k salary wasn't enough to pay 35k of expenses per year after taxes. Her response? "I don't care how much money I make. I will gladly live paycheck to paycheck. As long as I do what I love, the money doesn't matter." All the while, the entire class of first gens smiled and nodded in agreement and admiration.

If you are like this student, I commend and admire your compassion and commitment to your dreams. Such beliefs show that you feel a true vocation. However, I must be brutally honest and say every student that ever said "I don't care about money" regrets that decision. The money does matter.

The Money Matters

Right now, even though it might not feel like it, you have it made. Though you feel pressure to succeed, your goals revolve around grades and building a resume. If you need more money, you simply take out a bigger loan (which I would strongly DISCOURAGE, but go online and read more about financial literacy and why you should avoid college debt; *again, this is not financial advice)!

After graduation, however, your focus will (abruptly) shift from making grades to making a living and paying off debt (hopefully not much if any…). First, that living will revolve around providing for yourself. As a new grad you will need to make enough money to pay for an apartment, groceries, car, health insurance, and dozens of unexpected expenses. Not to mention none or a ton of student debt with terrible interest rates (look into this)!

Next, these individual responsibilities will evolve into more familial ones. You might have a family, take care of your aging parents, and deal with the continued increase of the cost of living (trust me… by the time you graduate, prices will be even higher). I share this not to scare you, nor to give you anxiety. Rather, I tell you this so that in 4-6 years time you do not look back and say "why did I choose this dead-end career. Living paycheck to paycheck sucks!"

Let there be no debate, no matter your love for your degree, if you can't make enough money to survive, your dreams will die. Whether you're the most passionate social worker, art major, or anyone, you will burn out. And burn out plus not being able to pay the bills in a few years is a dream killer. Disagree? Remember Maslow's Hierarchy of Needs from intro to psychology? Without money to pay for food (physiological needs) or rent (shelter), your professional passion (self actualization) dries up and eventually evaporates. You end up not having money to pay your rent, hating your job, hating life, … and eventually hating yourself! Sad, but painfully true. As brutally honest as this might be, my words come from a place of tough love. **Don't go to college to be poor.**

Remember that the goal is not just to graduate. The goal is to graduate with an in-demand degree and/or skills that will give you value in a profession you enjoy...or at least tolerate. Many first generation students, however, get this backwards. Many of us grow up hearing "getting your college degree is the most important." In the eyes of our family, any and all degrees equal more money and future prosperity.

This skewed understanding of college misinforms us on the connection between education and future finances. We approach college thinking "I need to get a degree in something I love, and hopefully it helps me make money." No. **The thought process needs to be "I need to** do something that 1) makes enough money, 2) I am talented at, and 3) that I love or at least enjoy."

Take it from your parents and learn to distinguish between a passion and a career. Many of our parents are manual labor workers and startup business owners. Do they love their jobs? Not really, and not usually. However, they chose a career that 1) makes them enough money to support their family, 2) is manageable emotionally, and 3) makes enough money to enjoy life OUTSIDE of work. When I see manual labor workers, they don't love their job, but they understand it is a means to an end. It makes them enough money to enjoy life outside of work.

We as first-generation college students have a luxury and responsibility our parents did not: the right to choose what to pursue. Having learned this, with this great power comes the great responsibility of choosing wisely about our career. Not all degrees lead to job security and many lead to lifelong stress. Even if you are on a full-ride scholarship for college, it is your responsibility to think about your finances after graduation.

Pursue a Career, Not a Hobby

Therefore, don't let your passions ruin you. Don't have financial "blinders" like so many first gens. Don't think passion plus persistence overcomes future debts. You might love dance or art (for example), but what's the likelihood of you making that a career? You might love fitness, but that does not mean you should aimlessly pursue kinesiology or nutrition. While both are interesting majors, they both pretty much require graduate school [college beyond a bachelor's degree] for any form of return on investment. Don't go get a kinesiology major just to become a personal trainer (something you could do without a degree). Have foresight. Look ahead. Plan out your career goals and review your options!

I share this because I was a fitness fanatic with the plan to study nutrition. I started out as a general nutrition major. Upon seeing that the dietetics-nutrition tract offered greater job opportunities and better pay than a general nutrition degree, I pivoted toward becoming a registered dietitian.

*To be fully transparent, dietetics is by no means a high paying career relative to other healthcare degrees such as doctors or physician assistants. Dietetics does, however, provide broad job options at the middle-class level, higher pay possibilities for top earners in specific sectors, and ample entrepreneurial opportunities. It also typically pays more than public health, wellness coaching, social work, and teaching jobs. Remember to always stay up to date on career outlook and median salaries by searching online websites. *

Then, during grad school (the 2 years after my bachelor's degree), I realized a PhD in Nutrition offered even more jobs and higher pay opportunities. So…again… I pivoted, not just in the direction of my passion, but toward higher financial and personal potential. (The sequel to this book will explain how I worked through my master's and PhD. Why? To not end up going to school to be poor.)

Looking back, I'm thankful I studied nutrition, then dietetics, and finally a PhD in nutrition/health behavior. It made me a unique and high demand speaker and job applicant with many skills. However, my advice to my younger self would include the following. Take off the blinders. Don't ignore your passion, but be open to exploring totally different majors. There's no shame in shifting toward higher paying plans. Talk to honest people (keyword: honest) that work in your "dream job." Are they happy? Do they feel fulfilled financially and personally? If they could start over, would they choose the same path? Find honest mentors and ask them these questions. You'll thank me later, no matter your degree!

In short: It's okay to go to school for something you enjoy (I hope you are fortunate enough to do so), but don't confuse your passion as a career compass. If it's not clear enough yet, the money matters. Take off your blinders.

Calming Your Nerves About Your Career

If you're feeling a bit nervous at this point, take a deep breath. You are going to be okay. No one has everything figured out from the beginning. It is normal to stress, self-doubt, switch majors, and even not work in your degree area. As a wise doctor once told me, "people think you have one career. But really, most people have 3-4 different careers during their work life. Change is normal and necessary."

As you experience the ups and downs of your college journey, remember your parents. Remember that as pioneers in an unknown land, they were once lost like you. Remember that they too felt stress, self-doubt, and had to switch careers over and over again. Even through these struggles, they too made it, and so will you.

Find parallels in your story with that of your parents to find solutions. If you change majors and feel like a disappointment, remember that our parents and mentors are experts at knowing when it is time to "abandon ship" (be it country or career). The generations before us laid the blueprint of success: stay a step ahead, think long term, work hard, make sacrifices, focus on your future, be open to change, don't be afraid to start over, don't waste money, be patient, and much more. We simply have to adapt these skills to the choices of our time. Once again, you were bred to succeed, so be passionate and be smart.

Aim to be a "Good Guy" That's Rich

At this point you're either thinking a) wow this guy only cares about money, or b) wow this guy really wants to open my eyes to avoid debt, be happy, and not end up hating the career path you once loved. Either way, if there's one thing you remember from this chapter, remember that it's perfectly possible to be BOTH a good person and a rich person (or at least financially stable). Having money does not make you good or bad. It's what you do with money that counts.

Stop viewing money as evil. Greed over money is evil. Wanting to be financially stable for your family and for yourself is not evil. Do you get what I'm saying? So many college students/organizations demonize the "rich." I know this because I lived and, thank God, overcame that phase too. We blame the rich for controlling too much of everything and for the evils of the world. Then we choose to stick with our financial blinders so we can avoid becoming "greedy and corrupt rich people."

Well, I'm here to tell you I'm thankful you have a heart, care about the poor, and promote environmental and social causes. However, do you know what the world could really use? THE WORLD NEEDS MORE RICH GOOD PEOPLE. The world needs people that limit college debt then have the money and willingness to change the world! You already have the heart to help, why not aim to have the finances too? That way you don't have to sit on the sideline and age in resentment. Don't go to college to be poor! Go to college to become a rich, good guy/girl!

So if you're a good person, for the love of God stop demonizing money. Money simply gives you the freedom to be more of who you are. It will allow you the freedom to donate more to charity, support small businesses, and maybe even open a successful business and provide good jobs! Therefore, if you're a good generous person, the world needs you to be smart with your money so you can one day change the world. Aim to be a good rich person one day. THE WORLD NEEDS MORE RICH GOOD GUYS/GIRLS. The world needs both. The world needs you.

In conclusion, as a college student, you have the privilege and burden of making a career choice. Don't take that privilege for granted. Find a career that combines your talent, fulfillment, and good finances. Know that your career can be a passion, but it's also a means to an end. It must be able to pay the bills, not mentally ruin you, and leave you with enough energy to enjoy where life truly is: outside of work.

Chapter 2 Summary

- Don't go to college to be poor. Use common sense.
- Avoid loans that put you into horrible debt for the rest of your life.
- Learn about debt interest rates and do some math.
- You should be building your wealth now. Stop waiting.
- Money does not make you a good or bad person. It's what you do with money that counts.
- Stop obsessing on hating the rich when you should be focused on making the best of yourself and your wealth.
- The money does matter. Aim to be, at minimum, financially stable.
- The world needs more good people to be rich. Why not you?
- See chapter 9 for more tips from other first gen college students.

I started this chapter by asking the question about your future salary. I finish by asking the question, "10 years later, with no savings, stressed for money, and bored of what was once a dream job, will the student who said, 'the money doesn't matter as long as I do what I love' please stand up?"

Chapter 2 Activity: Do Your Financial Homework

No one person/podcast will have all the answers for you. However, if you want "common sense" tips that go a long way, Dave Ramsey is a great start. Look up his videos on choosing a major, college debt, avoiding a university simply for their football or "prestige," common pitfalls, the danger of credit cards, and more. One of his videos that caught my attention discussed how most people with massive college debt are first gens that thought they were doing the "right thing" (financial blinders... remember)? Also try White Board Finance for a bit more in depth videos. The advice you seek is out there! Get informed.

There's a lot more to be shared on avoiding future financial ruin. The purpose of this book, however, is not about making you a financial expert. This book is not financial advice. You have to learn on your own or with a professional!

Take time to go through the money questions in this chapter and fill out the chart on the next page. Explore the finances of your career options. Go be a rich good guy/girl.

LIFE AFTER COLLEGE CALCULATIONS

Career Option	Median Starting Salary in Target City	Expected Monthly Income After Taxes	Your Expected Monthly Expenses	Potential Peak Salary
Option 1				
Option 2				
Option 3				

CHAPTER 3:
SETTING UP YOUR SEMESTERS FOR SUCCESS
How to Strategically Choose Your Classes and Professors

(Disclaimer: Make sure you know the grades (grade point average/GPA) you need to ensure your future success. Many majors are highly competitive. Some require a certain GPA to progress/remain in a certain track within the major (such as those that require you to attend graduate or professional school). These majors require students to be EXTRA focused from the very beginning of college. You can always improve your grades, but this is much harder when you start off poorly. Know your major and the grades you need.)

"All failure is failure to adapt. All success is successful adaptation." — Max McKeown

Now that you've (hopefully) chosen a career path toward financial stability, it's time for the real "core" of college: surviving each semester. As much as I loved college, I will never forget how I counted down the semesters left until graduation. Four years, eight semesters, one-hundred or so exams, and many sleepless nights stood between me and a life free from academic stress! (Little did I know I would continue on to a master's degree and PhD totaling 10 years, 20 semesters, countless exams, essays, and sleep deprivation. More on that in Book 2!)

The reality is, every semester comes with new challenges. Freshman year is about finding your place and surviving the weed-out classes. Sophomore year involves learning to balance harder courses. Junior year is overcoming burnout from the previous two years of school, with another 2 ahead of you (the glory of graduation seems so close, yet so far away). Senior year is about preparing for the future, but realizing you only have 2 semesters left to enjoy. My advice to you is simple. Don't count down the semesters. Make the semesters count.

The key to college is learning to set yourself up for success each semester. Take it from a guy who survived 20 semesters of college: there is a formula to success! Similarly, however, there is a formula that will lead you to flunk and "F" it up…as I did many times!

The first step to mess up your semester is to "bite off more than you can chew." By taking on too much, you prevent yourself from being able to focus on what matters: learning and getting good grades. High school success gives motivated students the false belief that you are ready to take on the world. The truth is, being valedictorian or top 10% does not equate to good grades in college. Many top 10% high schoolers actually struggle in college due to improper planning and… being overconfident.

You sit down with your advisor at your new student conference and tell them you want to take 18 credit hours (college classes vary from 1-4 credit hours per class depending on their time commitment; see your university website or advisor for more information). On top of this, you might say you plan to work full time, volunteer, and graduate with a 4.0 to get into medical or graduate school.

Though noble, this type of iron work ethic seen in many college first gen students, such as yourself, is also your greatest weakness. Vast dreams of success drive you to "bite off more than you can chew" and will lead you to failure semester after semester. You fail college because of lack of strategy and stubbornness, not from lack of intelligence.

Sadly, I know this from personal experience. During my freshman year my roommate dropped out of college, never to return to higher education. He was studying chemical engineering, was so smart and nerdy (respectfully). He was far smarter than me, yet, he flunked out of college. I'll never forget when he broke the news to me. I hadn't seen him in a few days and wondered where he was. One day, I returned to our dorm room exhausted from another long day of studying chemistry and biology. He was sitting at his desk and I noticed his stuff was gone. He said "Antonio, I'm going to withdraw from the university and move back home tonight. I kept failing my exams all semester, no matter how hard I tried. I didn't tell you because I didn't want to distract you (an honorable consideration given I was nearly failing 2 classes)."

Amid the shock and sadness, my roommate shared one silver lining. "The good news is, I have a thousand bucks left on my food card. I need to spend it all right now. Let's go to the college convenience store." While I was still in shock from the news, we happily walked to the store and bought as much as we could carry. We were two college students buying the "essentials:" beef jerky, string cheese, chips, candy, bread, and more. We purchased 600 dollars worth of groceries, possibly a school record! Then came the hard part.

Even though my roommate and I were not super close (mostly because we were both in survival study mode all the time), we had become good friends. We had both seen each other suffer, miss home, and struggle to assimilate as college freshmen. With grocery bags in hand, we said our abrupt goodbyes. It was like the movies: cold, gray, and rainy. He told me "Antonio, you're the best." Genuinely, I replied "nah man, you are. Go enjoy your family." I never saw him again.

How to Flunk College

The reason I share this story is because I learned so much from that semester where my roommate failed out of college. Not only did I learn why he flunked out, but also how I nearly did too. In summary, my roommate had transferred in from community college. He was a straight A student and was excited to begin university. Confident in his school-work-life balance, he registered for way too many classes. These included physical chemistry I, physics II, upper-level calculus, philosophy, and Texas history. He had simply "bit off more than he could chew!" (To this day I wonder if he chose to take too many courses, or if his advisor had persuaded him to take too many, or maybe a combination of both...either way there are lessons to be learned from this)!

Though he was bright and determined, he had so many classes that he failed every round of exams (he also played too many video games). Beyond that, he later found out he had selected the hardest professors for each of his classes. Subsequently, he discovered his instructors were either condescending, or simply did not match his learning style. Between work and long nights of studying he failed to make friends, so he has no social support with his studies. By the end of the semester, he was failing all but one class. After going home to visit his family, he'd talked with his dad and they decided that his best option was to drop out. Your worst nightmare, I know.

At this point, you're likely thinking "that would never happen to me!" The scary reality is, what happened to my roommate can happen to any of us. Sadly, my roommate dropped out thinking he wasn't smart enough to pass university. As I stated before, however, you don't fail college because you're not smart, you fail it because you lack strategy or because you're stubborn.

Learn the lessons from my roommate (and of myself that semester). Don't take too many difficult classes together. Learn the teaching style of your professors before registering. Adjust and improve on your study techniques each semester. Don't work yourself into the ground. Work smarter and not harder. Put simply: don't bite off more than you can chew. That's the recipe for failure, no matter how smart you are.

Strategies for Semester Success

Now that you know what not to do, here is the formula for how to succeed each semester. There are three basic rules: 1) choose the professor that will raise your probability of an "A," 2) balance your hard class(es) with easier ones, and 3) take the least number of classes necessary per semester (while staying on your timeline).

1) Choosing Your Professors

First, the professors you choose can make or break your semester. Choose a professor with a positive reputation, or at the very least avoid selecting the professor that all of your friends failed last semester. Investigating professor reputations is as simple as asking upperclassmen in your major about their experiences and advice. Additionally, though potentially less reliable, many websites allow you to look up grade distributions from previous semesters and comments from former students. Some include Rate My Professor, Rate My Teachers, ULoop, & Student Reviews.

Many of these websites also provide information on teaching style, the percentage of your grade made up of exams, in-class quizzes, assignments and presentations, and even attendance requirements. A more reliable source on course formatting and assignments, however, is the syllabus from the previous semester. Many universities require instructors to post their syllabus to the course registration site by a certain date prior to the semester. Thus, as a student you can go to your registration portal and look up the syllabus from the upcoming or previous semesters. In this manner you can choose a professor that relates to your strengths and that will improve your chances at an "A."

Put simply: when it comes to choosing professors, you need to first know your strengths and do your (pre-semester) homework. Don't be stubborn and just blindly go with what your friends, professors, or advisors tell you. This can backfire given that your "friends" might just want you to suffer with a professor like they did (aka these are not real friends). Similarly, most professors will encourage you to take their class. They, however, do not know your learning qualities. It's up to you to get online/speak with others to determine which classes best align with your strengths and learning preferences.

Don't do what I did and say "I'm going to get an A no matter the professor" even though the average grade in the course is a C. If I could go back I'd tell myself, "the name of the game is to learn and get high grades, while minimizing your suffering and stress as a student. So, for the love of God, learn your strengths and look up your professors! Stop being stubborn!" You'll thank me later.

2) Balancing Your Classes

Second, you must be conservative in your course load. During my first semester I earned 3 A's and 1 B. I then fell apart with 2 C's (borderline D's!) and 2 A's my second semester. Had I gotten less smart from semester one to semester two? No. Rather, I attribute my first semester success to my great advisor. She warned me "this is your first semester. I see too many smart students fail out when they take on two hard classes the first semester." Hesitantly, I took her advice and enrolled in chemistry 1 (my hardest class), philosophy, psychology, and a college prep class (my easy classes). Taking three easier classes (with instructors compatible with my strengths) helped me focus enough on chemistry to nearly achieve an A, and smoothly score A's on all my other courses.

The following semester I took both chemistry 2 (with the same incompatible professor because I was stubborn), biology 1, intro to nutrition (for majors), and anthropology. By the end of the semester I learned that my brain was not built to take two core science classes and their labs together. Similarly, I learned that my brain prioritized my love for studying nutrition to the point I failed to adequately focus on chemistry and biology. In short, I nearly failed chemistry, received a C in biology, and tanked my GPA all because I failed to set up my semester for success. Therefore, be conservative when you register for classes early on then build your course load up as you progress. Learn to balance your hard class with easier ones when possible. In all honesty... it will not always be possible (some semesters are simply semesters from hell), but do your best!

3) Less is More: Take Less Classes so You Can Focus More

One final consideration is to only take the minimum number of classes you need per semester (to finish on your goal pace). Rather than focusing on how many courses other students take, or what your advisor says (though their advice is important), focus on not stretching yourself too thin. Taking too many classes will lead you toward sleep deprivation, stress, the loss of your social life, and underperformance. Remember that you can take classes over the summer or as "mini-mesters" to lower your course load during the semester.

Furthermore, if you find yourself drowning mid-semester, remember to use your "class drops" as free "get out of jail cards!" Sometimes, dropping a class feels like failure, thus students avoid it. However, remember that dropping a class allows you to focus on your other classes and to (hopefully) achieve higher grades. Using your free course drops will also help you avoid having a "grade anchor" on your transcript. A blaring D or F can weigh down your future success and anchor it to a lower GPA.

Thus, don't be afraid to drop a class. Even if your professor tells you not to drop their class (and many instructors will discourage you from doing so even if you're drowning), do what is best for you. You know your situation better than they do. It may very well liberate you from a semester from hell! It will also allow you to choose another instructor or enhance your study habits for future semesters. Remember, dropping a class or taking less classes is not a "failure." Quite the opposite. Be smart and remember to choose your battles, and to not be afraid to lose the battle (dropping a class) so that you can win the war (graduate smarter and with higher grades)!

These three rules, though not comprehensive, are a basic template for guiding your semester planning. This might be the first time in your life where your semester choices impact your GPA and your dreams of an advanced degree. So if you're in a hurry to take on the maximum classes allowed per semester and graduate early, remember that the goal is not to suffer and obtain a low GPA. The goal of college in your life is to develop your knowledge and your whole self. Set up your semesters for success so you have time for the academic and social growth you deserve.

You are worthy of graduating college, not for your family, but for you and your dreams. You are smart! You are capable of doing well! But, you can "F" it up if you're not careful. Once again, don't take the maximum credit hours/classes your first semester. Remember, be strategic. Don't bite off more than you can chew.

Chapter 3 Activity: Reflect on Your Semester

After each semester you should take time to reflect on your performance. Why did you do well? Why did you struggle? How can you learn from this semester and improve? Below is a list of the things I learned each semester (S).

- **Freshman S1**: Take less classes than you think you can handle. Don't take the same professor twice if you already struggled with them the first time.
- **Freshman S2**: Don't take 2 super hard classes together. Make sure to have easier/fun classes to balance the stress. Don't sleep 3 hours the night before your finals. Don't eat a bag of Sour Skittles for breakfast before finals.
- **Sophomore S1**: When all the professor options are hard, it might be worth choosing the new professor and praying it goes well. You can always drop later.
- **Sophomore S2**: Only study as much as you need to. Value the power of sleep.
- **Junior S1**: Ask upperclassmen their "top tips" for upcoming professors/courses. Start thinking about life after college. What do you need to do the next couple of summers to set yourself up for success?
- **Junior S2**: Having a group of friends to study with (that won't distract you) will get you through those long semesters. Cherish them!
- **Senior S1**: Slow down and smell the flowers. School focused, but have fun.
- **Senior S2**: Finish the fight. Celebrate every small win! Have fun.

Now ask yourself: What did I learn last semester? How do I make next semester the best one for myself?

CHAPTER 4: EFFECTIVE STUDYING

How to Find the Motivation, Time, & Discipline

"If you're going to dare to dream, then you better dare to live the way that achieves that dream. How dare you dream and not live a disciplined lifestyle?" — Firas Zahabi

Do you want to know the truth about college? The truth is, the best part about college is also the hardest part. The best part about college is learning. The hardest part is also the learning! Early in my college career I realized that learning was AMAZING. I loved going to my physiology or nutrition classes and acquiring wisdom that would one day help people! I loved walking across campus on a beautiful morning and learning to see the world through the lens of philosophy or anthropology.

As much as I loved to learn, learning always came at a price! There's no way around it: learning takes a ton of time, brain power, and practice! As a bit of a "study-oholic," I remember implementing some excessively hardcore/weird strategies to learn. (Before I share these, remember I wrote this book in part so students like you could learn to work smarter and not harder like I did).

Freshman year I would study until 3 am the night before my 8am biology practicals. I'd then wake up with that horrible "headache, red-eyed, 'my whole body hates me' feeling at 6 am to crash study. (Ironically this strategy worked…until the day I overslept my alarm and had to sprint across campus to save my semester)! Sophomore year I'd lock myself in my bathroom for 2 hours at a time to study without distractions. Not to mention that, one time, junior year I entered the library at 9am on a Sunday morning and didn't leave until 4am Monday morning. For the love of God do not do this. To this day I feel like I lost a day of my life!

In retrospect, I studied more than was necessary in college. I regret not getting enough sleep, stressing too much, and locking myself in the bathroom for hours on end! Hindsight is 20/20, however, and at the time I was dedicating myself as best I could to my primary job as a student: to learn.

The reason I share these stories is because I hope you also dare to dedicate yourself to your dream. Know that learning takes work. College is hard. Hold onto your dream and the discipline to see it through. No matter your degree, the secret to college success is simple: love to learn and put in the work.

Staying Motivated to Study

One of the biggest challenges, however, is finding the motivation to study for 4, 6, or even 16 years as a student. Heck, it's hard to study for a single exam or a single semester from hell (gen chem, o-chem, or biochemistry anyone?)! In my case, as a first-gen student turned PhD, I studied and worked for just over 10 years! What's the secret to staying motivated? Years after my undergrad, during my PhD, I finally shared my "secret study motivation" with some freshman students.

I was teaching an intro level nutrition course. Before the first exam, a student asked me "Professor Miranda, how should we study for this test?" I told him, "when you learn about diabetes, write the name of someone you care about with diabetes at the header of that section. When you learn about heart disease, write the name of someone you care about with heart disease. Study like you're planning to help a person you care about. That's the key to success in any class." Be it psychology, business, medicine, nutrition, math, history, or speech, view everything as an opportunity to learn something to help someone. Most things you learn can and will one day be used to help in some way.

The "Love to Learn" strategy, however, does have some limitations. Many students don't feel a burning love toward their major or career. Additionally, every student will encounter multiple college classes along the way that are the opposite of love. There will be classes you will hate and simply aim to survive. For both of these scenarios, I want you to know-it's normal to "not be in love" with a career or to "fall out of love" or even hate a class.

While I personally loved to learn, I always admired the students that didn't obsess about school. These were the students that viewed undergrad as "the college experience." These were the students that didn't love their major, but they liked it "enough" and knew college was an important step in their life and career goals (see Chapter

2). They understood that the 4 years in college were simply another 4 years of life to be enjoyed. They attended class, worked hard, aimed to do well, but then relaxed. They enjoyed the moment, versus people like me that enjoyed the grind.

In summary, some students benefit from fully loving their major. Other students, however, benefit from a more tempered perspective. Whatever mindset you have, never forget to tie your studying to what matters: your future. Whether you love your class or not, remember to highlight and label your notes with your motivation. For some of you this will mean labeling your health notes with the names of your family and future patients. For others, this will mean writing "this class is terrible, but the degree will be worth it," or "every exam is a step toward a brighter future."

Always remember, what you learn matters. Maybe not now, but one day very soon, it will. Love to learn (or at least find purpose in it as part of your journey), and you will always have the motivation to continue. It won't always be easy. The love for learning, however, gives motivation to your work and will carry you through.

Finding Time to Study

In addition to passion, you must also stay prioritized, organized, and focused. In short, get the most important things done first, so that you may then focus on the less pressing ones. Many students study poorly because they fill their day with lower priority tasks (checking social media, emails, writing and rewriting a to-do list without actually making any progress on it), which impedes their ability to complete the high priority tasks (pending assignments, upcoming tests).

You feel "busy," but are not actually productive. You sat down to "study" for 4 hours, but actually only studied for 1 hour. By the end of the day your room is clean and easy assignments are done, but you inadequately studied for your big test tomorrow! The moral of the story is, keep the first thing first. Know your highest priorities and work on those rather than avoiding them.

One of my primary strategies was making a "plan of attack" to tackle my to-do list. I prioritized the list from essential (must get done today) to non-essential (if you don't get to it today then you can do it tomorrow). Next, I set aside a couple of uninterrupted hours per day to complete the main tasks. Turn off your phone, sit alone, turn on your music and get to work. Do not check emails or scour YouTube for 45 minutes looking for the right playlist (lowest priority tasks... aka distractions). Stop opening 20 tabs and going down useless "rabbit holes" of distraction. Focus on the task at hand. *An important note: if you feel like you can't ever get anything done due to distractibility, it may be time to visit your doctor. Many people have undiagnosed conditions. It is important for you to determine whether your distractibility is medical or due to discipline, environment, and stress. This is not medical advice. *

Designate certain times each day and week for your tasks and form a routine. Stick to your schedule as best you can. As you complete your tasks, check them off the list, and leave any non-essential ones for another day. It's okay to not finish your list every day, as long as you stay organized enough to rollover tasks to the future.

Effective Studying

Next, let your wins and losses guide the development of your study habits. When you have a successful round of exams, assess what contributed to your success. What was your routine? How did you organize the days leading up to the exam? How did your study habits influence your confidence for the exam? Similarly, when you "bomb" an exam or assignment, assess which practices hindered your success. Ask yourself what do I need to do better or differently next time?

Remember, failure is almost never fatal. Even if you don't do as well as you'd have liked, there is value in learning what does not work well for you. The highs and the lows are what eventually reveal the best habits for your future success. (For more on best learning strategies, I'd recommend looking into "types of learners and learning." You might find you do your best by writing, repeating, listening, or a mix of many strategies.)

Discipline in Studying

Lastly, if you've ever read or watched any self-help clip, you've likely heard that discipline trumps motivation. Discipline is training yourself to study habitually, no matter the circumstances or how motivated you feel. Discipline in studying is essential to your success. There will be days when you are not motivated, but you still need to show up (just be careful to distinguish between loss of motivation and serious burnout)! You're only as good as your routine, so stick to it!

Additionally, have discipline to IMPROVE your study habits. It's not just about showing up and grinding for 8 hours. Figure out how to make the most of your time. Become efficient. How can you finish those 8 hours of studying in 3-5 hours? Do you need more sleep, less study buddies, or less technology around? Find out how to get yourself into study mode faster and longer. Set up your surroundings. Get the right amount of sleep. Take a nap. Go for a run to wake yourself up or wind down. Know how often you need a break. It takes years of practice, but how great it feels to finally be motivated, disciplined, efficient, and focused. For more on improving your study habits, I encourage you to read or listen to the book Atomic Habits by James Clear.

Make Studying Fun

While I admit that I studied too much, what I don't regret are all the memories I made studying with friends along the way. I'll never forget having a "midnight breakfast" study break during finals. Nor will I ever forget my 19th birthday with a midnight library pizza party hours before our horrific chemistry exam.

Best of all, I'll never forget our late night library support system. We were all friends pursuing different degrees, but with the shared interest of genuinely caring for each other's success. We supported each other through the good times and the bad. Like you, we all had the desire to learn and one day serve the greater good as doctors, engineers, and much more. We were willing to sacrifice our time and brain in hopes of a better tomorrow for ourselves, our family, and the world. We were first-generation dreamers: stubborn in our determination and unwavering in our discipline.

With that said, get to studying! Study in accordance with your dream. Great dreams require great work. Embrace the challenge. Otherwise, a dream without a plan is just a fleeting wish that will never come true and whose absence will bother you forever. College is hard, but that's what makes it so dang special. That's what makes you special. We all have an inexplicable, unique calling to become the best at something. Whatever that thing is for you, go all in. Study and strategize with all you got and never be ashamed of your passion. Keep going.

Study Summary

- Tie your study material to what matters (your love for learning, helping others, or a career vision)
- Stay prioritized
- Reflect and improve on your study strategies and efficiency
- Stay disciplined
- Keep going

Chapter 4 Activity: My "Why"

Every first-gen student has a personal motivation to succeed. Take a few minutes to write a paragraph and reflect on your major motivators. Come back and read these during your hardest times or share with a friend/professional.

_____

_____

_____

_____

_____

_____

_____

_____

_____

_____

_____

CHAPTER 5:
STAY HAPPY, HEALTHY, & MENTALLY WELL

Avoid Guilt Studying
& Learn to Rest

"If you aren't having fun (at least sometimes), then you're not doing it right!" — Anonymous Toast Master (Toastmasters is a global organization that helps people improve their confidence in public speaking and leadership.)

The motivation of a first-generation college student is profoundly personal. Whatever your motivation, it is the source that drives the pursuit of your dreams. Dreams of crossing the stage and waving at your family up above. Dreams of walking with a diploma in hand as you bear your flag over your shoulders and a burning torch of accomplishment in your heart. Dreams of one day serving others through healthcare or business. If nothing else, the motivation to study arises from the dream of surviving another hellish semester.

Your motivation to work toward your first-gen dream, however, is both your greatest strength and your worst weakness. When taken too far, the motivation of many first gen students pushes us to "guilt study." While you've likely never heard of this word before, as a first gen, you know exactly what I mean. This is where rather than normalize a healthy school-life balance, we constantly work and study "because my parents suffered every day for me to be here."

Throughout my 10 years in school, I too suffered from guilt studying. Late nights and early mornings were the norm. I felt "lazy" if I did not feel exhausted from studying by the end of the day. Oftentimes I would look in my binder and say "I'll finally get to sleep more than 6 hours on March 8th (3 weeks away)!" Or even worse, during the hellish weeks of 3-4 exams I slept 3-4 hours per night for the entire week. I found myself struggling to stay awake during class, unable to retain my study material efficiently, and praying for good grades. What provoked such an unhealthy relationship with school and sleep was my guilt studying. I wanted to succeed so badly as a representative for my family. I wanted to honor the sacrifices of those who came before me.

As a first gen you likely sympathize with these feelings. Not only are we driven by personal success, but also because we grasp the magnitude of our collegiate opportunity. Opportunities not available to our immigrant or low-income parents and grandparents. By coming to university we have the opportunity to become a voice for our community, a representative for our dreams, and a flagbearer of education for our family.

Understanding this educational privilege we have as first gens drives many students to place excessive pressure on their shoulders. When it's late and you need to sleep, you tell yourself "if my papá can work in construction all day then I can stay up late to study." When you feel the freshman loneliness you tell yourself, "if my parents could start over in a new country then I can get over it." When you feel you should take a day off for the sake of your mental health you remember how your parents sustain a successful business without "any days off." You imagine their daily toil and use this daydream to enable your guilt studying. Trust me... I know.

Though imagining the struggles of our mentors helps us endure college, I hope you see that it can be mentally detrimental. Guilt studying causes us to ignore rest and self-care. Over time, our self-imposed guilt grind can lead to the deterioration of our social, emotional, and physical health. Overworking oneself leads to unnecessary suffering and worse grades and experience as a student. Sadly, many first gens recognize the need for rest and self care, but deprive themselves of it. Rather than rest, first gens relish in the warrior spirit to work hard to one day overcome... just like *mamá* and papá. Again... I know.

The Psychology of First-Gen Guilt Studying

Why does this culture of "guilt grinding" exist among first generation college students? As previously mentioned, many of us find ourselves trapped by the pressure and expectations we demand from ourselves. We guilt ourselves into late nights while thinking "if my parents could make it through their suffering then I should too." In a sense, the love for our parents, respect for our culture, and personal dreams lead us to a self-inflicted martyrdom.

You make yourself into a "first-generation martyr" to achieve the perceived ideals of our culture, family, and

American society. Our cultures of origin often ingrain values of grit and resilience. The self-sacrifice of our immigrant or lower-income parents indirectly causes us to idolize constant work. Since our parents made it through the American dream through decades of hard work, so must I. Simultaneously, American culture teaches us to always "climb the ladder." We learn to idolize productivity and maximal return on investment. These learned ideals, noble as they may be, are often taken too far into perfectionism, endless productivity, and burnout.

Overcoming Guilt Studying

How do you improve your relationship with school and self-care? Prevention of guilt studying begins by reframing how you view your heroes. Think of the people you idolize most for their sacrifice and success. No matter the person, be it your parents or a business owner, they prioritized rest. Though your brain might tell you "my mom and dad never rest and always work" the reality is they do rest. They likely sleep more and stress less than you. This does not make them any less heroic. It makes them human just as you are human. It also makes them smart because they recognize the need for rest to continue in hard work. Learn from their ability to prioritize balance. I promise, whether you sleep 3 hours or 8, the work will still be there tomorrow. Learn to put the pen down (ironic as I write this at 3am on a Saturday night).

Another way to combat guilt studying is to schedule your rest and fun. Yes, you read that right, schedule your rest and stick to it. Some students benefit from an entire day off each week. Others do better with a few hours of fun each day. No matter your strategy, take time to exercise, socialize, watch a movie with friends, participate in intramural sports, join a unique club, watch YouTube videos (with caution not to waste too much time), or pray. The homework for all students is to figure which routine of rest works best for them. Remember: a constant grind drains the mind, but a rested mind makes it to the finish line! Be intentional about your rest. Plan your time off.

Thirdly, I encourage you to listen to your body and to use common sense. Remember that the human body is not supposed to live in constant sleep deprivation and stress! Use common sense and go to sleep before your brain is fried, otherwise you're wasting your time. Eat your vegetables, take your vitamins (as needed), and for God's sake go outside. Spend time in the sunlight, with nature, and to get your eyes away from the screen.

If I could go back and give myself advice, I'd say the following: "Stop studying at 110% effort, when you can achieve the same grade with 90-100% effort. Stop wearing self-sacrifice as a badge of honor. Get some freaking sleep, kid." In a society that idolizes self-sacrifice and dedication, choose to only work as hard as you need. Any work beyond what is necessary to accomplish a goal is simply self-defeating pride or people-pleasing.

Stay Mentally Well

The final point about rest is that you must take it seriously. Years of hard work led me to constantly "guilt grind" far beyond my undergrad and into my PhD. I had snowballed responsibilities of work, research, homework, teaching, volunteering, and writing. I ignored my fatigue and burnout. How dare I listen to my body in pursuit of my dreams? How dare I get 8 hours of sleep? Instead, I falsely reprogrammed my brain to relish in that false "badge of honor" that is the guilt grind.

I'm here to tell you, as a recovering (and constantly relapsing) workaholic, work never stops until YOU learn to stop. Otherwise, your body will force you to stop. As you will read in great detail in the second book of this series (Diary of a First Gen II: Graduate School), the years of school, burnout, and sleep deprivation led me to develop high blood pressure, anxiety, and a year of panic attacks. After all my dedication, my greatest strengths as a first-generation student, hard work and devotion, had become my demise. The guilt grind came at a heavy price.

For now, just know: losing your mental health in pursuit of any dream is not worth it. Like I said before, if you can achieve your goal by giving 90%-100% effort and enjoying life, why go 110% and hate life. I know you will likely be stubborn like I was. You won't listen like I didn't listen, but for once in your life kid, give yourself a break. Your work is not the same as your worth. You're worthy of rest. You're smart enough to give yourself time off. To rest is to trust in your abilities. Trust yourself. Get some dang rest.

In conclusion, embrace your role as the flag bearer of education in your family. Take motivation from the heroic efforts of your mentors. Learn from their ability to balance work and rest. Stop thinking you need to suffer because you "owe it to your family." Embrace the grind, but don't suffer unnecessarily. College is hard enough. Don't make it harder, by demanding too much of yourself. Don't make yourself into a first-generation college martyr like I was. Normalize rest and appreciate every day of your life. If you're not having fun (at least sometimes), then you're not doing it right!

Chapter 5 Activity: Plan Your Self-Care

Below is a table of examples of self-care behaviors across multiple dimensions of health (left column). Choose a minimum of 1-2 areas you need to improve (we typically neglect at least one area of our health). Then circle/write in what your daily and weekly goals are for that week. For example, my area of neglect was always emotional. In my case I'd choose 1) listen to a funny (non-school related) podcast during my walks for my daily goal and 2) meet with a therapist (universities often have free therapy or college coaching) to learn work/life balance for my weekly goal. Get to work rest!

Health Dimension	Daily Self-Care Examples	Weekly Self-Care Examples
Mental	• Sit in silence for 3 minutes • Journal before bedtime • Set your maximum study time • • • •	• Plan a study free day (or afternoon) • Schedule a counseling session • Attend a retreat • • •
Physical	• Exercise $\geq$30 minutes • Sleep 7+ hours/night • Stretch/Yoga • Go on a walk • • •	• Plan your meals for the week • Go on a long walk/run • Try a new fitness hobby • Sleep in! • See a doctor or dietitian • • •

Emotional	• Practice deep breathing • Creative outlets (art, dance, etc.) • Journal • • •	• Meet with a therapist weekly • Play with puppies at a dog shelter! • Goat Yoga! • • •
Social	• Call someone who always makes you laugh, or brings you peace • Join a club of people with shared interests! • Spend quality quiet time with others • • •	• Plan a weekly social event (make it a tradition to look forward to!) • Volunteer for a good cause • Attend events that are out of your comfort zone (but not dumb ones) • • •
Spiritual	• Pray for 3-5 minutes • Say/Write what you are thankful for • Read for 10+ minutes • Spend time in nature • • •	• Attend weekly service • Volunteer at your home of worship • Help others through your faith • Surrender to what is out of your control • • •

For more information on health and wellness, please visit my website. There I have 45-minute nutrition courses on weight management, type 2 diabetes prevention, and diabetes management for you or a loved one. Remember to seek in-person professional help if that works best for you.

https://www.antonionutrition.com/work/courses

Alternatively, scan the QR code below:

CHAPTER 6: BUILDING YOUR SUPPORT SYSTEM

How to Build Relationships That Will Help You Grow

"A friend is someone who makes it easy to believe in yourself."

–Many

The underlying theme of college, and of this book, is simple: grow your independence. It is now and forever your responsibility to take care of yourself as best you can in all aspects of life. From waking up to your alarm and showering at a socially acceptable frequency, to budgeting your money, setting the trajectory of your career, picking yourself up when things don't go your way, handling love, loss, and breakups: the world is now yours (no pressure)!

Thankfully, part of becoming independent is realizing the key to college and life success is to not go it alone. Learn to cultivate a good support system. Find supportive friends, social groups, academic mentors, and network with people who inspire you to think "I want to be like them when I grow up."

Don't Make College a Solo Journey

If you feel intimidated or exhausted by the idea of building a support system, then you are not alone. Whether you are an introvert with a small social battery, or an extrovert with insecurities, we all struggle with making and keeping the right friends. As an extrovert with a limited social battery myself, I struggled with balancing school and social life early in college. Making friends was difficult for me. Not because I was shy, but because my approach to college was "off."

I entered college as if it was a "solo journey." I saw college as me against the books, and friends would somehow come along the way. I'd been spoiled in grade school where friendships didn't require work. You simply show up to the same place with the same people every day from elementary through high school! Up until college, I never needed to "work" to make and keep friends.

This "solo mentality" made my first year a bit lonely. I was always happy, but mostly alone. At freshman camp I made acquaintances, but was not really looking nor expecting to make lifelong friends (partially because I already had some back home). I stood back and cringed as everyone chanted the freshman camp cheers. I was a nonconformist and anti-peer pressure to a fault. I didn't want to be "brainwashed" or "try too hard" to make friends. Even once school started, my biggest "mistake" was not putting in enough social effort. I met and made acquaintances in every class and on every walk, but didn't try hard enough to make them into long-term friends. I was good at making conversations, but poor at making connections.

Not knowing how to put enough social effort into friendships led me to spend much of my first freshman semester alone. The friend groups I did make were super fun, but I often excluded myself because I was "too busy" with school or training for a marathon I had signed up for. My first roommate was from Korea and had his own friend group. My second roommate flunked out, which left me to study alone in my dorm most of the time. My best friends in my dorm were the janitors and the pigeon that nested outside my 3rd story window each day while I studied. Even then, my favorite janitor friend changed jobs, and one day the pigeon stopped showing up at my window.

Alone Amid an Ocean of People

There were two major events that eventually opened my eyes to stop being an individualist and non-conformist. First, was when I went home for a visit a month into college. While home, I ran into my friend's mom. She immediately asked me "have you made your lifelong friends yet?!" Unwanted questions often force you to confront the things you avoid.

I remember thinking "Why is this clueless lady asking me this? How the heck could I make lifelong friends a MONTH into college?!" To this day I would still say it's rare to meet your "friendship soulmates" a month into college. That conversation, however, got me thinking "maybe I should try a bit harder to make friends."

The very next week I challenged myself to grow in school spirit and meet some people by going to my first college football game! It was an incredible experience! My parents hadn't gone to college, so I had no affiliation nor intensity for college football. This lack of expectation made the game all the more amazing. I remember walking up the endless stairs surrounded by an ocean of people in maroon and white. We all stood shoulder to shoulder in a stadium filled with nearly 100,000 people. The sound of chants and cheers booming through the stadium on every play for 3 hours is indescribable.

Though it's a bit sad to write about now, I went to that first football game by myself. In a stadium full of 100,000 people, I was alone. I didn't know anyone. It was also a rainy game, and I hadn't packed a poncho. Every touchdown celebration was a relief from my wet shivering. Though I celebrated with the people packed around me, a deafening stadium was not the best place to make friends. For the first time in my life, I felt insecure as I realized everyone in the stands, in some way or another, was there with a group: friends, couples, dorms, frats, sororities, organization, etc. then... me.

Though a bit sad to read, don't feel bad for freshman year me! Rather, I hope you find wisdom on what NOT to do. My loneliness was my own naive and stubborn fault. It was self-inflicted solitude due to my excessive independence. I simply didn't know that to become truly independent is to learn how to connect with others. I learned- the hard way.

I share with you my most vulnerable moments, so that you can live a better, more fulfilling college life, from start to finish. All of my isolation could have been avoided if I was more open to making deeper and genuine connections with individuals, groups, and organizations from the start. All of my isolation, however, led me to learn and now share my experience with you. No regrets. You live, you learn, and you pass on your wisdom.

The Right Friends Will Find You... If You Put Yourself Out There

The irony of that dreary and lonely football game is that it was the same day I met one of my best college and lifelong friends. After the game I attended a hangout for first-gen students (God bless organizations that support first gens). I made friends with some guys over barbecue tacos and talking about our hobbies. We all liked Superman, science, and...tacos. It was such a simple moment, but a genuine one among some first gens just trying to make college work. We all exchanged numbers after eating and hung out thereafter.

From that day forward I discovered people that genuinely wanted to hang out with me. While I didn't know it at the time, just a week after being blinded by the idea of not yet having genuine college friends, I had found them. Looking back, that was the day I learned that you're not always meant to find your friends. Sometimes, if you have the courage to put yourself out there, they find you. In my case, they found me when I needed them most. Thank God.

Finding Genuine and Supportive Friends

A lot can be said about how I evolved from a freshman without a group to a senior with many friend groups. The truth is we all have our own journey and timeline. Put yourself out there, but don't feel pressured to desperately make friends. Better alone than in bad company. Be open, but honest. Conversely, learn to give people a chance. I, like everyone, at times "judged a book by its cover." Many of my best college friends came from random events- a bus ride, doing laundry in the dorm, suffering in science classes, bravely sitting next to a stranger at the cafeteria, and much more. I'm forever grateful that they gave me a chance to be their friend and that I gave them a chance too.

Importantly, find friends that become reliable study buddies, compliment your study strategies, and that don't distract you (too much at least, you should still have fun)! Make friends that challenge you to be better both in school and in life. Compete with each other, respectfully, but have each other's back. Most importantly, choose friends that will support you through the good times and the bad. Those that will celebrate with you when you do well, encourage you when you want to quit, and simply listen to you when you have the worst grade or day of your life. Real friends listen, if and when you choose to open up. Those are the real ones.

Beyond Friendship: Building a Future Network

It is also important for you and your academic friend group (those with similar career goals) to get involved with and learn through organizations, internships, upperclassmen, professors, conferences, and volunteering. Whether you're aiming for an awesome job (as you should) or an advanced degree after college, learn from those on that same trajectory. Surrounding yourself with other like-minded people will help you determine the steps necessary and whether you are on the right track to reach your goals.

Only through working with and listening to others in your target field will you find the best "roadmap to success." Find out if you need an internship, a certain GPA, work experience, etc. Put simply, don't "reinvent the wheel" when the roadmap is already drawn by others! Together you will know more and achieve more.

College Friendships Final Tips

In summary, the worst thing you can do is make college a solo journey. Don't deprive yourself of the friendships that await you after high school. Many of your lifelong connections will come from going off to college, if you put yourself out there. No matter how silly or scary, no matter if you feel like you don't belong, get involved. Stop being comfortable. You have undeveloped and untapped sectors of personality in your brain that will only grow if you challenge yourself socially. Don't box yourself into who you were in high school. Don't count yourself out of making friends.

Aim to make friends (or even just one) that genuinely care for you and wish the best for you. Likewise, aim to be the same for others. Importantly, give others a chance, but be mature enough to recognize when someone is leading you down the wrong path of drugs, dullness, envy, or even danger. Additionally, recognize when you've outgrown a friendship or relationship. Always keep an eye out for when a connection is leading you to the garbage can (emotionally, mentally, spiritually, or physically) instead of the promised land.

As you can see, building your support system and professional network can be uncomfortable. Learning to make connections, however, is the foundation of your future success. Most of your future jobs will come from who you met (or didn't meet) in college. Best of all, most of your college memories won't come from your hours alone in the library. Rather, your college memories, I hope, will be filled with amazing experiences from your connections that challenged you to be more and do more (just not drugs, of course). Get involved, have fun, and always aim up. Life awaits.

Chapter 6 Activity: The Definition of a Good Friend

I wanted to share a few of my favorite quotes on friendship. Sometimes, a quote speaks more than an entire chapter. Enjoy!

"Life is partly what we make it, and partly what it is made by the friends we choose." – Tennessee Williams

"You are the average of the 5 people you spend the most time with" – Jim Rohn

"Your network is your net worth." – Porter Gale

"As iron sharpens iron, so one person sharpens another." – Proverbs 27:17

"A real friend is one who walks in when the rest of the world walks out." – Walter Winchell

"A real friend will tell you the truth even when it hurts." – Many

"A friend is someone you can tell bad news to and they won't tell you why you're an idiot, and they won't interfere with your suffering. They'll just listen and maybe they'll suffer along with you. And they won't tell you about some worse thing that happened to them. They'll listen [to you]. But a friend is also someone you can tell good news to and the friend will say 'wow in this veil of tears (life), something good happened to you. Great man- wonderful! It's rare. It's unlikely. Good for you. I hope 10 more things like that happen.' And they're not envious, jealous, or one-upping you." – Dr. JBP

CHAPTER 7:
BE YOUR OWN BEST "HYPE MAN/WOMAN"

How to Build and Rebuild Confidence in Yourself

"The brain simply believes what you tell it most. And what you tell it about you, it will create. It has no choice." — Shad Helmstetter, What to Say When You Talk to Your Self

No matter your personality or friend group, college is a time to grow your confidence and to learn from your setbacks. My first time nearly flunking a class in college was the greatest struggle of my academic life. After being a straight A student in high school, I couldn't imagine getting a B in a class! Ironically, my first B in college came my very first semester at the mercy of an ungodly Gen-Chem class (have I mentioned I hate chemistry?). Going into my second semester, I was prepared to achieve straight A's once again, but life had other plans.

No matter how hard I studied, I failed every chemistry and biology exam my second semester. Looking back, that was a semester where I'd chosen the wrong professors and had bitten off more than I could chew (see Chapter 3)! Walking into my finals, however, I still had faith I could salvage a B in these classes. I couldn't imagine the chance of getting a C or even less failing. Two days later, I was dejected to find out I'd failed both final exams (Gen Chem with a 42 and Biology with a 68)! If I'd have missed 1 more question on my chemistry final, I would've failed the class and biology was not much better.

After that 2nd semester, I was in the dumps for weeks. I'd gone from all A's my whole life, to feeling like a total failure for myself and my family. I felt incompetent, helpless, burnt out, and frustrated. I felt... DUMB. "If I can barely pass chemistry 1 and 2, I'm never going to graduate. I'm going to drop out. I'm a failure." In all honesty, I even went to the local community college website and considered applying in preparation for flunking out (a bit of catastrophizing but that's how scared I was)! I had lost all confidence and felt ashamed.

A week after nearly failing college, amid my mental struggles, I attended my cousin's college graduation. During the ceremony, I had that "pit in your stomach" emotion: a mix of anxiety, defeat, and shame. As I witnessed each student cross the stage, the thought of my own graduation felt like a distant fantasy. "That'll never be me," I told myself sadly. I felt I would never graduate, and I would fail at making my family proud.

Life, however, has a way of sending you help in the most random of ways. After the graduation we all took pictures of joy and celebration! On the surface I smiled, but internally I'd lost all my confidence from nearly failing. Amid my silent internal struggle my aunt and her friend approached me. My aunt introduced me and unexpectedly said "This is Antonio... he is the smartest one in our family."

At that moment, as I heard my aunt say "the smartest in our family" I felt time slow down. Though insignificant to everyone around, that phrase resonated with me and woke me up from my cloud of self-doubt. In a moment where I had lost all confidence in myself... a single sentence of positivity saved me. Though she didn't know it, my aunt Angela made me believe in myself once again. Whether I was the smartest or not did not matter. What mattered was that someone still believed in me, even when I didn't believe in myself. And in your hardest of times, that's all you need.

How You Talk to Yourself Matters

The reason I share this story is because college is the time to work on your self-talk. Going into college I had very positive self-talk! After nearly failing freshman year, however, my brain was stuck in reverse! I had almost all negative self-talk. I couldn't stop beating myself up mentally, until my aunt's encouragement brought light and life back into my clouded brain.

The ups and downs of college taught me that healthy self-talk (a mix of positivity and accountability) is essential to your academic and overall success. Why? Because as you will learn in your freshman psychology class about the "self-fulfilling prophecy": *who you tell yourself you are, is who you will likely become.* Do you tell yourself you are smart and worthy of success, or do you say you got lucky and don't belong? In a weird way our self-talk reveals our self-fulfilling (positive) and self-defeating (negative) beliefs about ourselves. Whatever you tell yourself, remember that your brain believes you: so speak kindly.

Improving Your Self-Talk

Changing your self-talk takes time, but it is possible! First, identify the source of your self-talk (why are your thoughts always self-defeating or self-promoting). Self-talk is partially a product of how people have verbally treated you throughout your life. Were you frequently told you were smart, pretty, and the next superstar? These words stick with you and form the framework of how you view and talk to yourself.

In times of need your brain repeats these words to you. "I am smart. I am worthy. I am pretty inside and out." Over time, these words of encouragement become lifelong personal mantras. They become your self-talk! Most importantly, having this positive self-talk is the difference between being humbled or crumbled during the hard times ahead.

If you find yourself thinking "I definitely am not kind to myself in my self-talk", you are not alone! In fact, you are probably in the majority! Many students grew up in a life where they were discouraged, belittled, or even traumatized. "You can't even mop right! Why can't you do anything right! Stop asking so many questions! Why are you so dumb?!" Sadly, such experiences scar us for life. The self-doubt from others leads to self-doubt from ourselves. From a young age we begin to think that we are not smart, pretty, or ever capable of the goals we set for ourselves. Rather than having a mind of encouraging self-talk, we have a self-defeating one.

The great news is that these words, experiences, or even wounds of trauma are not irreversible! The beauty of understanding the power of words of harm or healing is that we get to choose which we share with ourselves today. Perhaps my best piece of advice in this whole book is to grow into your own best hype man/woman.

In my case, I forever held onto the phrase "I'm the smartest in the family." During my darkest moments during the next 9 years of school, my brain somehow always recalled this mantra in times of need. When I felt nervous before giving a presentation or doubted myself in front of "smart people," my brain always remembered, "he's the smartest in our family." No matter the challenge, that mantra always gave me the strength to overcome. I'm forever indebted to my aunt for those words. As for you, find your mantra, hold onto it, and cultivate your positive self-talk.

Be Your Own Best Hype Man/Woman

How do you go from simply collecting mental mantras to becoming your own best hype man? The answer differs from person to person. Just as a lifetime of discouragement has a harmful effect, a shift to encouraging thoughts, over time, can and will heal. Heal yourself by complimenting yourself. Hype yourself up after passing a "little" quiz, for acing your exam, for having the courage to try and "fail." (In reality, you never "forever" fail, you either win or you learn. Your setbacks are an experience to learn from, not to beat yourself up about.) The more you celebrate the "small victories" the better your brain becomes at believing in future success. Dare to be kind to yourself. You'll thank yourself every day of your life.

As someone who's struggled with self-confidence, I'd encourage you to make celebrating every "small victory" a habit. Compliment yourself for daring to ask a question in class, getting a question right, scoring better than last time, or acing a test. Each and every time you doubt yourself, yet achieve it, compliment yourself and never forget it. Over time you will gain confidence, learn to expect success, and be more stress free. You will come to learn that expecting success is not arrogance, but a sign of self-worth. Eventually your positivity will snowball into a healthy balance of positive self-talk and humility.

Relax and Rebuild Your Confidence After Setbacks

In summary, I know what it feels like to feel like your entire future rides on one exam. More importantly, I know what it feels like to have failed that exam and to end up okay. That C in freshman gen chem was the last C or B of my life! Ironically, it was the best thing that could have happened to me. That "C" taught me how to study better and choose my professors more wisely. Though hard, nearly failing built my grit and resilience and to believe in myself no matter what.

It also taught me perspective. One exam or class, in the grand scheme of life, is not the end of your world (though it ALWAYS feels like it). If I could go back to my sleepless and struggling freshman self during those times,

I'd read him this chapter. I'd simply tell him, "you're gonna be alright kid. These setbacks are more secret ingredients to your success. Keep working. Keep showing up and always speak kindly to yourself."

In conclusion, your past does not define you. One class or failed exam does not define you. What people say/said about you or made you believe growing up does not define you. Your anxious and negative self-talk does not define you. You are more than your anxious thoughts. The beauty of college is that YOU DEFINE YOU. Be kind to yourself, encourage yourself, and seek help. Narrate a beautiful story of encouragement, humility, and self-care in your brain. Be your own best hype man. Work at it. You can do it. You deserve it.

P.S.

It is important to mention that it is normal to struggle with negative thoughts. The struggle between confidence and self-doubt is what makes us human. If you are struggling, know you are not alone. Becoming your own best hype man/woman takes time and support. Be it your family, friends, or a professional, don't be afraid to ask for help. Learn about the therapy/counseling resources from your university or through alternative sources.

Chapter 7 Activity: Become Your Own Best Hype-Man/Woman

It is time to practice healthy self-talk. We tend to be more encouraging to others than toward ourselves. Write in how you would react to/support a friend going through the following scenarios.

Failing a test:

Passing a test:

Struggling with a change in major:

Going through a breakup:

Nervous before finals:

Remember to treat yourself the way you would treat your friend. Be kind and show grace to yourself. When you go through these experiences write down how a friend would support you...then talk to yourself like your own best friend. Be your own best hype man/woman!

CHAPTER 8:
FOCUS ON YOUR GOALS, BUT ENJOY THE MOMENT

How to Plan for the Future, While Enjoying Your College Experience

"Get out there and enjoy it. It goes so fast." — *Dr. John Delony*

All the advice in this book might make you think "college seems like a lot of work!" The reality is, college is a lot of work, a grind, stress, highs, lows, wins, losses, and many other things. It's a mixed bag of experiences and emotions. Welcome to the rest of your life.

The fact that your life (which won't always revolve around college) will always be busy and semi-stressful (at "best"), and traumatic (at "worst"; because all challenges, eventually, help you grow) was summarized by one of my professors. Halfway through the spring semester of my sophomore year, my nutrition professor noticed how stressed the class appeared. She asked us "what's going on today? Where's the energy?" A student next to me replied "we're tired. We're always studying and working and always busy." She replied, "you're always going to be busy. Life is busy. The busyness never goes away."

At that moment I didn't think much of the advice. The older I get, however, the more real her quote becomes.

Your whole life will be busy, and it's up to you to make time for yourself. College, grad school, your first job, marriage, raising kids, grinding to make enough money, saving for retirement, and even retirement; it's all busy. Life never slows down, until you slow down.

Therefore, the sooner you come to realize that your life will always be busy, the sooner you can break free from it. Realize that though life is always busy, how you manage your time makes it manageable and enjoyable. Learn to add breaks into your schedule for things you love and need. I mean this (adding time into your schedule) both literally and figuratively. Make/block time on your schedule for adequate sleep, fun, friend time, prayer, meditation, relaxation, quiet, no-cell phone time, cooking, and yes even goat yoga (Google it) or pet play time (see Chapter 5). Whatever you need to stay balanced and sharp mentally/physically, make time for it. Change your approach from always busy, to always balanced.

Make a Bucket List

A helpful trick to help you stay focused on all of your academic, future, and fun goals is to make a bucket list. I made bucket lists for my senior year of college and it served me in two ways. 1) It kept me focused on academics and on enjoying/accomplishing fun experiences! 2) It taught me about what I truly valued and most enjoyed in life. Some people use a vision board (Google it if you are not sure what it is). Either way, you need a list of goals and experiences to accomplish before your time in college is up. Otherwise, you will just float along and miss out on some great opportunities both socially and academically.

See the activity section at the end of this chapter for my senior year college bucket list. (If you really want to get into the psychology of happiness and purpose, I encourage you to listen/read the works of Dr. Arthur Brooks, PhD).

The Real Purpose of College

The essence of the college experience involves two themes. First, college is the time to start building toward your career and life goals. It's where you choose your career, find your talents and passion, and mature socially and professionally. It's the time to put in THE WORK. Find a passion, a purpose, and a plan to get there. Don't stay idle. Your future awaits. Put in the work.

Secondly, however, college is the time to slow down and enjoy the moment. One of my favorite psychologists, Dr. John Delony says "it (life) goes so fast. Get out there and enjoy it." And it's true. College is but a blink of an eye in your life: four years (or 6 or 10-12 for my masters, PhD, and healthcare professionals) out of 70-100 you'll likely live. Though a short period in your life, it's important not to rush yourself through these college years.

Work toward your goals, but learn to LIVE LIFE. The best thing you can learn in college is learning to live. Life isn't found hating every day and wanting college to be over. Rather, life is found in the overlooked beauty of everyday moments. Life is going to freshman events and meeting a lifelong friend over a brisket taco. It's staying up until 2 a.m. studying at the library surrounded by classmates for moral support. Life is sitting next to a pretty girl or cute guy during the first week of class and getting to enjoy their company the entire semester (and who knows... maybe far beyond)! It's noticing someone that's lonely and walking with them after class to let them know they're not alone.

Life is telling an anxious friend "you're the smartest person I know" and seeing the smile on their face. It's about waking up late for an exam and sprinting across campus to save your grade. Life is about going through difficult times and calling home and crying on the phone with your mom, dad, or siblings and discovering how deep their love and support are for you. Life is pancakes for dinner with your friends before finals because everyone's run out of food!

It's shaking your professor's hand after turning in your final exam and sharing a mutual grin of respect (either because you kicked their a$$ or they kicked yours)! Life is spending time with your roommates on a Friday evening and going out on a Saturday night, or planning a spring break trip with them. Life is daring to study a semester abroad because NEVER in your life will you get that opportunity (this is your sign to study abroad). It's about starting an intramural team even though you're no good at the sport, because... why not?! Life is watching a sunset over the campus and enjoying every season of the year. It's about struggling and finding yourself spiritually both independently and through community.

Life is about going through tough times. It's about being wrecked emotionally due to a tragic death or breakup and coming out a better person. It's about losing a friend to suicide, yet uniting as a friend group to carry on and enjoy life just as your friend would have wanted. Life is about selflessly becoming a mentor for younger students. Life is going through highs and the lows and discovering the truest version of you.

Life is going through all of this and then getting to graduation day, crossing the stage, pausing to take it all in then staring at your family in applause. It's living that moment and celebrating not just the degree, but the journey that got you there.

Though lengthy, I hope this narrative summarizes your college and life's goal: to get to work, but enjoy the moment. Love to learn, but learn to live. Don't just make school and career happen. Make LIFE happen. You'll thank yourself later.

Chapter 8 Activity: The "Bucket List"

Many people make a "bucket list" (a list of experiences or accomplishments before you "kick the bucket" [aka before you die/leave somewhere]). My senior year of college I made a bucket list to remind myself to work hard in school, but to enjoy life. Below you will find my original list!

Notice my bucket list includes academic, future, professional, and fun stuff! This list helped me sprinkle in fun, fitness, faith, and friends amid the chaos of college! It also kept me focused on my goals for the semester and grad school. Additionally, it felt GREAT every time I crossed something off. A little pat on the back to help me become my own best hype man. Most importantly, it helped me stay balanced. Life is always busy. We still have to enjoy it.

SENIOR BUCKET LIST
(Antonio Miranda, Texas A&M University, Class of 2016)

Travel/Sports

- Tour 3 nearby cities
- Go to an away football game
- Go to one game of each sport
- Study abroad one semester
- Visit a new state
- Plan a spring break trip with roommates

Miscellaneous

- Make a "day trip" out of my drive to visit home (stop at a restaurant, landmarks, go on a hike, visit the small towns in between, etc.)
- Have a group picnic at the park for my birthday
- Sit in on a philosophy class
- Write a thank you letter to my favorite professors
- Participate in all campus tradition events

Competition

- Run a 5k
- Compete in intramural sports
- Win a food eating contest
- Take a fun exercise class
- Get into the best shape of my life (I'm not getting any younger!)

Goofy/Fun/Food

- Fridays = favorite shirt day
- Dress up as Superman for the Halloween football game
- Try a new restaurant each month
- Go to the local festivals
- Have a picnic in academic plaza
- Try a new haircut

Service/Growth

- Help someone in need
- Mentor younger students
- Volunteer to clean the church for 3 hours

Quality Time

- Spend time with family
- Visit each roommate's hometown before graduation
- Have a semester with Fridays off!
- Have a day at the lake

Academia

- Pass the graduate school exam/get into grad school
- Get straight A's
- Internship
- Pass math class

CHAPTER 9: TIPS FROM PREVIOUS GRADUATES

Navigate College:
Money, Mentorship, & Mindset

(Disclaimer: Remember that every respondent experienced college in their own unique manner. We all faced unique barriers and circumstances. Each response highlights a valuable recommendation, but may not represent the best advice for your specific circumstance. I, personally, do not fully agree with the totality of each response, and some responses actually counter each other. However, I included all the responses to give you a broader range of suggestions and to "paint a better picture" for the endless circumstances you may face. Remember to seek help for your specific situation from trustworthy mentors. These responses do not constitute financial, mental, or any other form of legally binding advice. Remember to one day pass on your wisdom, as we have done here.)

"As you are now, so once was I. As I am now, so you will be."
— Roman Epitaph

It is an honor for me that this chapter is a collection of wisdom from previous college graduates. I sent out a survey that humbly asked "in less than 3 sentences, what is the best college advice you would give your younger self/a current first-gen college student?" With genuine enthusiasm nearly 100 college graduates responded: all with the goal of helping YOU, the next generation of first gens. Below are their answers, categorized by themes. I pray and have faith that you will stumble across the advice you seek when you need it most.

1. Check how long your scholarships are good for. Many universities give you a lot of scholarships the first year (to get you in the door), but then less the following years. Read the fine print on your scholarships.

2. If you aren't entirely sure on what you want to pursue as a career, don't feel pressured and rush to start college right away after high school. Getting life experience, working/saving money, traveling and meeting new people might inspire you to pursue careers and fields you never even considered possible. Accumulated debt from a degree in something that you later realize isn't your ideal career might bog you down from being able to switch later on.

3. College provides a unique skill set but not all skills require a college degree. It is more important to figure out your purpose and figuring out the skills you need to obtain those goals than blindly pursuing a college degree and hoping it will make your life better.

4. Once you're graduated and in your career, no one knows or cares about where you started. If community college is your best option at first, do it then transfer to your dream college.

5. Shadow different professions before choosing your major.

6.   You can work a blue collar job and still be very successful in life.

7.   Study whatever you want in college; not what your parents or family members want for you, but what you want to study. Trust me, you'll be happier and closer to your chosen path.

8.   Go shadow and talk with people who are already doing the careers you think you want. What do they like and not like about their chosen career? Do you like the daily tasks involved with that career? Find the career you think you want first by shadowing all sorts of jobs during your first year of college or even before, then go get the qualifications from college required to do that job. This will save you money in the long run and give you a job you KNOW you will like in the end.

9.   Take advantage of application fee waivers to save money, fyi all "free and reduced lunch" students qualify for it. Submit your FAFSA EARLY, talk to your parents about the information you'll need. Even if your parents are undocumented you can still submit one.

10.   Focus on what brings you joy from a content and learning lens combined with what has a practical, financially positive career trajectory. You should enjoy your field and what you do, but don't let it define you. Remember: you can always learn new things on the side or extra for fun. Be willing to

pivot or change course during your career, that's where true growth happens.

11. Make sure you're choosing something you love. There will be many challenges with money, relationships, time, etc.; but, if you are passionate about your major, then it's worth it. If you don't love it, then don't do it.

12. My mom gave me great advice, "love won't pay the bills." Consider if what you're studying has the potential to support the lifestyle you desire. Be sure to study a subject that is useful, you will have plenty of time in your life for passion projects.

13. College is not for everyone and it's not worth getting into debt for a useless degree. Times are changing. Don't feel pressured to follow the traditional route.

14. Don't go to college just because you think it's what you're supposed to do. You can find more success on other paths if you aren't pursuing a particular vector of research.

15. Make sure you choose a major that makes money and has growth too. Growth keeps you motivated, while stagnation dries you up. Real talk.

16. Imagine what your life and career will look like over the next 10,20, and 30 years and ask yourself if you think you will regret the decisions you make today, tomorrow? Use your youth and freedom to invest heavily in the skills and relationships that can help

you make better decisions. Life only gets more complicated.

17.   I would say to make sure that you are informed before going in, making sure that you can afford it and if not what options are available to you. With that being said, college is supposed to be fun, as first gen students we are focused on working hard and breaking barriers but we should have fun along the way just like everyone else.

Be Financially Smart: Stop Caring About What Others Think & Start Saving Money

18.   You need to change your mindset on money from a young age. Learn a skill while you're young that people will pay you to do in the future (manual work, artwork, speaking, business, sales, coaching, teaching, etc.). Then, in high school make sure you get a job and start making or saving money. So many of us as first gens are taught the wrong mentality. We are told, "don't work extra or you will be taxed more." This is the wrong mentality. Yes you may get taxed slightly more, but you will make more money now versus not working. (Example: you work all summer and make 12k and are taxed 2k [12k - 2k = 10k for you to save] vs you don't work all summer and make 0 dollars.) We are also told "work after you're done with school" (WRONG). You should be thinking about savings, 401k, investments, house/rent prices etc. from the time you graduate high school (or before). Save money every month if possible (imagine if you

saved 20 dollars a week during high school, now imagine if you saved 200 - 2,000 a month in your 20's.) Snowball and grow your money every year. Life isn't getting any cheaper. Make and save money now.

19.   College is not free. I remember scheduling my first semester and the advisor told me "how are you going to pay?" I had no idea.

20.   Credit cards are not free money. You need/should pay them off at the end of the month. Learn the basics. Build your credit. Don't build bad habits.

21.   Three rules: 1) minimize debt to fund your education, 2) pick a useful major with longevity in mind, and 3) complete an internship to make you attractive to prospective employers.

22.   Any class that you can knock out at the community college for pennies on the dollar, DO IT! The most affordable option is not the worst option; it's the practical option!

23.   Understand what career options you will have with the major you choose. Be realistic about picking a major that will provide you with opportunities that will satisfy your needs (including financially). If money matters to you then don't get a dumb degree and if money doesn't matter to you then just know you have to be realistic about the kind of lifestyle you'll have post-college if you end up in a career that isn't financially lucrative. Final thought: If you

don't intern in college you've done something wrong.

24. Do a lot of research on getting scholarships for first gen students. Make sure you don't have to pay the scholarship back in the future.

25. Get a door to door sales job to graduate debt free.

26. I would say: only go to college if you need an advanced degree like nursing, or to be a doctor or something like that. Instead, focus on what you are passionate about and what you wanna be or how you wanna be or what comes first, or what kind of life you want to build. Next, I would try to build a business to combine my passions. The truth is: people that don't know what to do when they go to college end up wasting a lot of time and have a lot of debt. Instead, find a business that you love that you are passionate about and build it. One thing we are taught in school is how to be an employee. No one teaches us how to run a business so I would find a mentor that I would like to be like that makes all the money that I wanna make and that is the person I want to be like, and tell them that I want them to mentor me. A lot of times first-generation kids' goal is to go to college, but what happens is you get debt and don't learn real life skills. Your real life skills are learned in the real world. In conclusion, build a business and don't be an employee.

27. This journey, whether it be college, life, or your career is all about balance. Advice, suggestions, etc. come from all over, but it's you that has to balance your yin to your yang. Have fun, but don't go overboard. Commit, but don't burn out. It is all about balance. That is where longevity lies.

28. Prioritize your health. Prep meals or have easy options to eat, make time to move (even if it's just 10 minutes), and go to bed on time! You cannot handle stress effectively and think clearly without taking care of your body.

29. Exercising, having fun with friends and family should not make you feel guilty, try to find a balance.

30. Create some sort of consistent routine or schedule for yourself outside of your classes. One that involves hobbies that get you out of your dorm room. Library study days, workouts or walks, clubs or groups, etc. It can be easy to create a habit of staying inside your dorm room and it can be hard to break. It's important to rest too though, so create a good balance of both!

31. Work ethic and a positive mental attitude will always prevail. Advocate for yourself and learn to practice self care. Sleep is important; it's better to think clearly over content you know and be able to critically think over that which you're not familiar with than to be foggy due to your sleep deprivation

with both content you know and aren't familiar with.

32. Don't be too hard on yourself and remember to give yourself time to recharge and recover so you don't overwork yourself!

33. The college years can be overwhelming, I would suggest focusing and taking one semester at a time.

34. FIND YOUR IDEAL SLEEP TIME and stick to it. For years I slept either 4 - 6 hours per night because I was lying to myself that it was enough sleep. I felt terrible all of the time. Years later I found out I felt awesome with 7 hours and stuck to it! Slightly more sleep changed my life: feel better, retain info better, do better!

35. You won't regret working hard. You will regret working too hard (aka you will burnout in your career at a younger age). If you can get an A with 90-100% effort, stop giving 130%. Take it easy. Live balanced, not busy.

36. Stop living on 4 hours of sleep per night. It's horrible for your health and makes you way less efficient.

Stay Organized

37. Always read the syllabus and understand the class's grading system.

38. If you have classes that let you go at your own pace, always stay one week ahead in case things in life

pop up. Also, this allows for you to ask instructors questions and gives them ample time to get back to you with an answer.

39. When scheduling your classes, keep in mind the distances between buildings and locations. Ten minutes between classes may not be enough time to get from one place to another. Allow yourself time in between and really look at a campus map when scheduling classes so you don't end up running back and forth when you don't have to.

40. Stay at the library and finish your work before you go home. What are you rushing home to? Getting home with the peace of mind that your school work is done is not just about your grades but also your mental health.

41. Pace yourself. If you go too hard with your volunteering and people pleasing and doing a million things for your major and professors, you will hate your field by the time you're 30. Get involved and gain experience, but don't overwork yourself or you'll lose your soul to work hard down the road. Pace yourself. Stop being a people pleaser.

42. College students should sleep early instead of staying up all night. In addition, use good time management rather than procrastinate before a test or an essay to better prepare you for staying ahead of important meetings or deadlines in the workforce.

43. Learn to adjust your study strategy. My main goal was to stay up late 2 nights before the exam (maximum study time) then sleep a decent amount the night before to be fresh the day of the exam. It usually didn't go as planned so I learned to always be able to adjust my study timeline. Desperate times sometimes called for desperate measures (never did and all nighter but close! Try to avoid them as they're a sign you're simply not ready or waited too late to start studying).

Work Harder & Smarter: Build Great Habits Early

44. College is HARD WORK. Work hard. Dreams come at a price. Go after them!

45. You're there to study. It's easy to lose focus and motivation. Celebrate accordingly but practice self control in all ways.

46. College life, especially for a 1st generation student can be a culture shock, both academically and socially. It's easy for one to get distracted or bogged down by the happenings on and off campus. My advice to one is to remember why you're there in the first place. The first year is always the hardest and if you let yourself become distracted, you'll end up having to climb a mountain of your own making. Focus on your studies. first-generation students will always have to work twice as hard to reach the same amount of success as students that are to the manner born. Never forget that.

47. Don't let this (being a first-gen) define you. You will have to work harder but you can and will exceed your peers after putting in the effort.

48. Find out how you best learn and study early on. Try different study methods until you find the one that best helps you. Having discipline early on will be your guide these next four years.

49. You might feel like you have to work twice as hard than people who grew up in a scholarly family. And that feeling might be true. Take that as an opportunity to build and strengthen your grit and work ethic.

50. I know it's hard to carve your own path especially when it seems others had it handed to them. I promise your hard work will pay off and your success will be even sweeter.

51. There's so much pressure. Your anxiety attacks, your refills each month, the professors don't care, your family doesn't understand, I get it. Just know this will soon pass. Just do the best YOU can. Don't go home right after classes. Don't meet up with friends right after class. Go straight to the library EVERY DAY and STUDY for at least two to three hours. THEN go home or with your friends. Treat that as a nonnegotiable. Emergencies are people dying. If no one is dying, stay in that library and STUDY. Not social media, not on the phone. STUDY. Set yourself up for success. Your anxiety will thank you for it.

52. My advice to current college students is to think about how much their future self will thank them for showing up and doing the work today.

53. Don't be afraid of failure. If you aren't doing things in college that push your limits to almost failure, you're not doing college right! Take risks, take chances, and be a 'yes man!' You only live those years once!

54. Learn to speak and write professionally. It's time to grow out of the lazy slang language (that's fine while you are around your friends) and learn to master reading, speaking, writing, and thinking. Email your professors professionally.

Mentorship: Build a Community for a Better College Experience

55. Take time to talk with as many people as you can, whether that be professors, friends, staff, new people you meet through events, etc. There is always something to learn through someone else's journey. Keep an open mind as you go through college. Your goals may change, and that is okay and totally normal!

56. Find your community in college whether it be through a club or church (I did both!). These people and their support will carry you through joyous and difficult times. I now have found a family in College Station and back home (Gig 'Em Ags!) I wouldn't have survived college without my communities.

57.   Speak up! Don't be shy. As a first generation, one thing that held me back was a fear of speaking to others, especially my professors. I always assumed that I would be okay by just going to class and doing the work, however, I realize now that opening dialogue with my educators, counselors, and co-workers would have made my first-generation college student experience a whole lot better.

58.   Ask questions and find your staff ally (they might not be first gen but they see you)!

59.   If you are having academic issues, reach out to an advisor. If they aren't able to help resolve the issue, go see a different counselor at the advisors office. Sometimes getting a different perspective can better help you get past big barriers that hold you back.

60.   Don't be surprised by anything. A college education is "a team sport." With new resources, you'll figure it out.

61.   Never underestimate the power of relationships both personal and professional and put forth a valiant effort to grow them. Always go to office hours if you're not making sense of class, they often will reward that extra effort.

62.   Seek out Role Models: Connect with successful individuals who share a similar background as yourself. Seek a lot of advice from older students, professors, or professionals who can guide and inspire you throughout your college journey.

63. Go into college ready to take in advice and wisdom from as many people as possible. Talk to as many people as possible to get to them and their stories.

Friendships and Relationships

64. Surround yourself with people who love you, and you love back. Reach out for any and all types of help, especially if you feel your mental health is at stake. Take the time to enjoy college life and the new connections you're bound to make, instead of speeding through it.

65. College is overflowing with different groups of people that all have their own goals they hope to accomplish in college. From one first gen to another, surround yourself with likeminded people that will propel you to be better rather than steer you away from your identity. Personally, I found my people through a college ministry, and I will always cherish the long lasting impact they have left on my life.

66. Join different organizations, the people you meet in them will become lifelong friends.

67. Find a good support system. FAMILY, CHURCH, FRIENDS to study, etc.

68. Eff that guy! Chase your dreams! Your dreams don't wake up one day and decide they don't love you anymore or cheat on you. Stay true to yourself.

69. Remember why you started. Don't let a gf/bf deter you from your goals. Find a supportive partner that

wants you to achieve your goals, with or without them.

70. Stay out of a relationship unless you are truly in love. If your spouse is dictating who you can and can't hang out with, that's a poor relationship. Go out, meet people, and figure out what you want.

71. If you keep losing all of your friends, the problem might not be them. It might be that you would benefit from a therapist or counselor. Don't isolate during tough times. Isolation + mental health crisis is a recipe for disaster. Seek help.

Professional Development: Open Doors Through Networking & Experience

72. Make as many connections as possible! Your future career will be shaped primarily by the people you know, so network and meet as many different people as possible by going to events or volunteering for different groups. And networking shouldn't be transactional. Make an effort to create meaningful relationships with people from all walks of life.

73. Never underestimate the power of connections: Devote a good part of your time in college to networking and forming solid and long-standing professional relationships with people who work in the field you aspire to join after graduation.

74. Attending college is a challenging journey, which can test your confidence, patience, and financial

status. However, it is important to be resilient and find what works best for you. Always have a positive mindset and find opportunities to help move you forward, such as having mentors, finding volunteer opportunities, working part time jobs, and joining student organizations to help open your network.

75. Utilize your relationship building to leverage Aggie networks. Don't discredit anyone; you never know which connections may open doors.

76. Resources and opportunities are ubiquitous; you just have to find them and say yes.

77. Network! I made this mistake and it has affected me after graduation, network and make sure to apply to internships!

78. Push yourself to experiences you might not feel ready for (like a leadership position, or volunteering in a new place). I feel like I learned the most in areas where I pushed myself and didn't necessarily feel ready for but it helped me grow so much and see after completing them what I am capable of, which helped with my confidence.

79. Do as much networking as possible because you never know if the person sitting next to you will end up being your best friend, business partner, boss, or a future employee.

80. Network, network, and network some more. We all know that going to college and getting the degree is

valuable. But I believe that the relationships you build in those four years can go a long way to shaping your professional career. That friend, professor, TA or counselor could lead to your big break. Remember that each relationship you build is one degree of separation closer to where you want to be.

Personal Growth

81. College is a one time experience at a young age. If you go, balance is the key. Enjoy the experiences, but don't overindulge. Balance. Participate, but don't overcommit. Balance. Slack off and have fun, but don't throw in the towel. Those who know how to balance have the greatest success in my opinion.

82. If you have confidence, grit and resilience you will be successful. Confidence to trust yourself and what you want. Grit to put in the work and resilience to overcome.

83. We are programmed sometimes to figure things out on our own since we should only rely on ourselves to solve problems we face. I thought if I asked for help while in college that I was admitting I was stupid. I quickly learned that asking for help is a strength, not a weakness.

84. It's okay to ask for help when needed; seeking assistance is a sign of strength, not weakness.

85. College is a time for you to figure out what the world has to offer as you prepare for this part of

your life journey. Discover your passion and take advantage of the opportunities that different schools and organizations are offering for you to fulfill your dreams. Do not be afraid to go against the grain and fail as failure will only help you be a more rounded individual.

86. No matter the stress or fear that may come from the unknown, it's worth finding out the answer to that unknown in the end. The personal journey to that end goal, no matter the length of time, is an important piece to your growth.

87. Rarely does anyone have EVERYTHING figured out (although many people you may meet portray it so). This is a crucial time in your development as a human being, and part of figuring out who you are & who you want to be involves CHANGE. Embrace change.

88. Take the time to get to know yourself better. Improve your self-discipline, self-efficacy, and intra and inter-personal awareness. Understand your stressors, motivators, and triggers to help build future meaningful connections.

89. If you believe, you can achieve. Even the slightest amount of confidence can get you somewhere.

90. Always say yes to a challenge or opportunity. You never know what will evolve from it.

91. 1) Do an extracurricular that you're really interested in and really invest yourself in it. The experiences

(especially leadership or when you had to make tough choices) make great talking points in a future job/internship interview. 2) Start to think about where (city/state) you would want to end up after graduation. Start establishing your network there. Build up those online connections (LinkedIn). 3) Don't compare yourself to your peers. You're writing your own unique story. No one has walked the journey that you have. Be proud of every step that you take even if it's a winding path.   4) Find the professor that really enjoys their job and cares, they'll love lifting up students and being their advocate and really allow them to get to know you and your passions. They're the ones that will spend hours working on your letter of recommendation, they'll send you job and scholarship information, they'll sit with you when you're making tough decisions, and when you graduate they'll be there cheering you on.

92. Run towards your fears and challenges because that's how you grow. Don't take anything for granted; always do your due diligence. Set yourself and the next person up for success.

93. Have a solid vision or goal that you can work towards. Be disciplined, have a strong work ethic, but most of all be grateful for the opportunity you have.

94. Don't count yourself out because you're "too cool" or box yourself into limitations. Be open to trying new things even if it seems silly.

95. You're not always right.. don't be a know-it-all.

96. Don't be afraid to reinvent yourself and step out of your comfort zone and do something you have never done before. College is really a diverse melting pot of education, culture, experiences and opportunities that you could have never imagined. Try it all over the next four years until you find what's right and meant for you.

97. You are a product of several generations of your family's love, support, and efforts, but remember to chase YOUR dreams, not your family's. At the end of the day, your family wants you to be happy and successful, but those are measured in many ways outside of prestige, job stability/security, and income. College not only provides you with knowledge and a degree to prove you know how to do something, but also life experiences to help you discover your passions and niche within society.

98. College is a time to grow up and grow out of your bad habits. No one is perfect, but it's important to avoid/stop habits that will sabotage you for life. Stop "people pleasing," stop talking bad about yourself, stop gossiping, stop wasting time on addictions, and many other things. Start enjoying life, enjoying hard work, finding purpose, building healthy relationships, mentoring, saving for the

future, and much more. Learn to confront yourself. It's never too late to change for the better. Your life's just getting started!

99. Always say yes to a challenge or opportunity. You never know what will evolve from it.

Words of Encouragement/Recovering from Hard Times

100. Don't stress about being the smartest or the best in the room, because if you're either of those things, you're in the wrong room.

101. Dream high, and don't let yourself feel you crashed down with the first bump. Enjoy the journey and take every challenge as a learning experience.

102. If you are smart enough to get accepted to that college you are smart enough to graduate. DON'T DOUBT YOURSELF.

103. Think you are doing this degree for your future! It takes effort and sacrifice, but it is worth it! Maybe people around you do not understand and it is ok! Keep going!

104. The stress, struggles, and sacrifices you will confront are part of the path you are forging for yourself and your bloodline. Have faith that the actions you commit to today will be felt for generations to come. I am proud of you.

105. No matter how hard it gets...no matter how discouraging the journey feels...keep going!

106. If I could talk to my college self, I would encourage her to know that everything she thinks she can't accomplish, she can. Her future self appreciates the hard work and perseverance.

107. Often, with time comes clarity; don't stress if you don't have all the answers after your first semester or first year because there will still be a lot to learn.

108. "GO FOR YOUR GOALS NOW. You might fall in love or choose to get married early on in life and you may never again get the chance to get whatever degree(s) or career you always wanted (or it won't be as easy). Family and having kids is the best thing on Earth, but make sure you achieve your other major goals too so you can have the best of both worlds and set yourself up for success in the long run. Life is a series of ever closing windows. Your opportunities come and go faster than you think. Get the degree. Go for the dream. Connect with people. Go for it NOW.

109. Although things might not be easy and you feel like there might be no guidance as to what to do. Do not give up, pursue your dreams and do not let the financial aspect deter you from accomplishing what you want from life. It's an investment and your future self will thank you.

110. After your dream big, dream just a tad bit bigger. We're all capable of more than we think we are. Push yourself.

111. "Do it for your whole self. You can be successful academically but take care of your emotional, mental and physical self to truly embrace the fruits of your efforts in the end.

112. No matter the challenge and obstacles, if it feels right, go for it, trust your gut no matter the outcome; being a first gen student is about learning as you go.

Enjoy the Journey: Have Fun, Meet People, & Live in the Moment

113. Take the time to enjoy life around you instead of focusing on getting through it and finishing. Build those relationships and have some fun.

114. Do not sacrifice everything social just to study. You will NOT remember that "A" you got on that one test 10 years from now. You WILL remember the memories you made with people.

115. Find and get involved in something that stimulates you socially. I spent the majority of my college experience doing two things: going to school and working as many hours as my school schedule would allow so I had a savings cushion when I graduated. And while obviously, working isn't a bad thing, don't forget to chill out a bit and find people that you can relax and recharge with.

116. College will lead you to believe you have to take only the mandatory classes to finish school quickly. Don't fall into that trap. Take electives and use this

time to grow yourself and find hobbies that you might enjoy.

117. Most importantly enjoy the journey, I had a non-traditional college career that took me longer and I felt very alone during the process as a first Gen college student. While it may seem like a lot, enjoy your time and have fun, I wish I could go back and appreciate those less adult responsibility days more.

118. Go to class, take advantage of having practically zero responsibility, and have fun with your friends.

119. Go out more! This is the time to find yourself and not just stick to books and work. Find and make time to start that convo, meet new people, and try new things you never have before!

120. Slow down. This is the only time you get to be a true college student with limited responsibilities. Take that spring break trip SOMEWHERE! For the rest of your life you will HAVE to work, enjoy the experience.

121. Make your happiness a priority. Sure we're doing it for our parents, but it's also your life. And you only get to do it once. You'll never get to have the true college experience again as a young, naive college student.

Honorary Mention

122. *"A good leader knows how to follow."* –Miguel TAMU Class of 2016

CHAPTER 10:
FULFILLING THE DREAM OF GRADUATION & BEYOND

How to Lay the Path for
the Next Generation

"Education is what remains after one has forgotten what one has learned in school." –Albert Einstein

As you near the end of your college years, I hope you reflect on your amazing journey. Think of all the amazing things you've done and the challenges you've overcome. Remember your younger self and be proud. The eager freshman you once were, will appear like a distant memory, an entirely different person. As you walk around campus those last few months, remember where you made friends freshman and sophomore year. Every corner of your university will whisper memories that trigger you to relive the good times and the bad.

In those final months, you will pause and stare at your old study spots. In a daze you will recall the exhausting hours of study and sleepless nights. The sight of the chemistry building will remind you of your first failed test. You will remember the feeling of having failed an exam, wanting to call home, but suffering in silence because you didn't want to disappoint your family. You will remember the professors that supported you but also those that crumbled your confidence. These memories, as arduous as they might be, you will cherish forever.

You will view the younger students confined to their books and cubicles. You will feel compassion for those students starting the difficult journey you have now nearly completed. Oddly, the sight of exhausted freshmen will fill you with a bit of nostalgia and the desire to relive the highlights of your college adventure. You will then quickly snap out of that longing to relive the past when you remember what a relief it is to have the "all nighters" of studying behind you (unless, of course, you're going to grad school)! Above all, seeing the younger students will make you appreciative of your challenge-filled journey. That exhausted student was once you: alone, confused, and praying to pass. Imagining your younger self will bring emotions of pride for having overcome every challenge and surviving every transformation. You did it.

The Secret to Success: The First-Generation College Code

While reflecting on your journey, you will inevitably come to the conclusion, "wow, how in hell did I make it?!" The answer, in part, is that you were born from pioneers. These heroes, our parents and mentors, sacrificed their youth in search of opportunity. For many, the motivation was not a dream, but rather survival. The need to survive and provide for their families led them to travel across deserts or oceans. In a foreign land they adapted to a new language, culture, and currency. For decades they toiled toward a dream. Not in hope of lucrative success, but because it was what needed to be done to survive.

Upon pondering the experience of your parents and mentors, you come to realize that the story of a first-generation student mirrors that of these hard-working heroes. In the face of necessity and poverty they chose hope and opportunity. Likewise, in fear of stagnation ("peaking" in high school) you sought self-actualization. You too crossed a desert. One of mental solitude and academic hardship. You too faced rough seas that brought you to your knees and nearly sank your (mental) ship. In a foreign land (college) you too struggled to form a community amid an intense culture shock. In a foreign land you mastered a new language (your major), culture (expectations), and currency (knowledge). For years you toiled toward a dream, in hope of success.

Given these similarities, many students will attribute their success to "my parents. I wanted to make my parents proud. To make their sacrifice worth it." Though honorable, the reality is, you did not make it through college because of your parents or mentors. Rather, you made it through college because of an inadvertent calling to follow the first-generation college code. The code to honor the sacrifice of those who came before you through your own strenuous journey. You willingly chose to put in the work because you knew the value of hard work not just for yourself, but for your family, and the generations to come.

When seen in this manner, you realize that you were not born a pioneer. Like your heroes, you honorably and courageously chose to be one. You chose to honor the first-generation college code. Within you lies a spirit, work ethic, an…inexplicable *ánimo* (a Spanish/Latin word for morale, enthusiasm, and life force, my favorite word) instilled generations before you. What the world considers a first-generation "disadvantage" you now understand to be the greatest advantage of all. You did it. Stay humble, but be proud.

Helping the Next Generation

As you prepare to move on from college remember to always pass the first-generation spirit forward. Start by mentoring the next generation. Be it a friend or family member, encourage them just as you once needed encouragement. Help them make smart choices. Tell them you believe in them.

Choose to be good toward others. The world is full of people wanting to be great. But what the world really needs are people who choose to be and do good. Work hard. Don't betray people. Have a servant's heart. Be the salt and the spice that the mundane world needs. Be a hope. And don't forget, when you are rich or at least financially stable, give back charitably. My fellow first gen graduate, it's your turn to help others. Lay the path for the next generation.

Graduation: An End and a Beginning

I am not sure when in your college journey you will read this book. But, if you've read this far, you probably daydream of crossing the graduation stage as your family cheers. As for me, my undergrad graduation was one of the best days of my life. Yes, it was hard because it marked the end of an incredibly fun era filled with constant new experiences. But graduation was also amazing because it symbolized the overcoming of all the challenges described in this book.

I remember leading up to graduation I was afraid something would go wrong and that I would not cross the stage. I kept going to my long-time advisor's office to check that all my requirements were complete. After visiting him for a third time he closed his laptop and said "Antonio, you are graduating; you made it. Just enjoy these last few weeks. Stop worrying. The work is done." I had been working so hard for so long that I couldn't believe it. The work certainly was done.

Perhaps most humbling, was that so many of my family members drove into town the night before my graduation. Many of them were the unsung heroes behind this book. My parents, who through their hard work, inspired me to work hard. My sisters who did my FAFSA for me when I was a young procrastinator. My cousin Omar, a great mentor and who was the true "first in the family" to set the bar high. My cousin Jessi whose graduation inspired me to try again after nearly failing my freshman year. My cousin Gerardo, who once listened to me vent and shared a sincere "don't give up, dude." My hardworking and loving *tías* and *tíos*. And of course, my aunt Angela, who's comment "he's the smartest in our family" became my internal voice for years to come.

On the actual day of my graduation, I woke up ecstatic even after only 3 hours of sleep. I was the first one in line before the arena doors even opened. Once the commencement ceremony began, the girl next to me tapped me on the shoulder. Amid the sea of thousands of graduates in maroon and black graduation regalia (most of them bored and ready to get the ceremony over with), she had noticed my atypical excitement. She asked me "are you first gen? Is that your family up there?" We both turned and smiled toward a group in the crowd where 30 people wearing blue Superman t-shirts smiled and waved back. My sister had coordinated for everyone to wear the same shirt in honor of me always wearing a Superman shirt to my exams. I smiled and appreciatively replied "ya… I'm first gen." Words cannot describe that moment of pride and gratitude.

Next came the graduation stage. I'll never forget the feeling of joyful nerves of anticipation before crossing for my diploma. Before my name was read, I looked up at my family. Then, as my name was called, I pulled open my graduation attire and showed my Superman undershirt, not in arrogance, but to show humility. To show that it was not just me crossing the stage. It was all of us. It was for everyone wearing a Superman shirt that day. As you too will learn, though only one person crosses the stage, symbolically you walk for the generations before you and the many or the special few who helped you along the way.

As I posed for a picture with the dean, he looked at me and said, "your family sounds very proud." Little did he know that as proud as they were of me, I was and forever will be even more proud of them. WE did it. Thank God.

Among Many First-Generation Graduates

What also made graduation incredible was knowing that my fellow first gens and classmates also made it. So many of them have stories that should and could be written. Stories far better than mine. Some of my first gen friends had matured at an early age due to the early and tragic loss of a parent. Many of them grew up in single-parent households or in poverty. Others faced the constant pressure of paying for their school, while also supporting their family emotionally and financially back home.

Many arose from years of family trauma and mental health struggles. There were first gens that during college lost a lover to heartbreak, a father to cancer, or a friend to suicide, yet still carried on. Wow is all I can say. These were the first gens who were and to this day are my heroes.

The first gen stories are endless and deserve to be told. For now, I hope my story does the first-generation struggle some justice. No matter our background as first gens, on graduation day we were all the same. We had finally done it: from first-generation college students to first-generation graduates. What an honor it was, is, and forever will be to have graduated as a first-generation college student.

Your First Gen Journey Awaits

In closing, I am proud of you. Just like the thousands of first gens that preceded you, your achievements are to be admired. Be proud of yourself. Never take your accomplishments for granted. Your journey is what has prepared you for the future. Soon you will enter the uncertain oceans and deserts of the world once again. This time, however, you will know you were built to go forth and pioneer. Remember everything you've overcome. Knowing the struggles and successes of your journey you can go forward confidently into your future. Courageously pursue your dreams amid the challenges. Never forget to have fun. Be humble, but unapologetic in your big dreams. Aim for your highest potential.

Your success will forever be a tribute to those who came before you and those who look up to you. Being first gen is a great mental advantage to have in life. You're used to being the first; keep going. From first-generation college student to whatever you choose to be. Therefore, dream big, win big, and love big. Save, strategize, and succeed. But first, my friend, slow down. Cross that stage and celebrate like never before. You've earned it. God bless you on your journey. I'm proud of you.

ADDITIONAL RESOURCES

I hope you enjoyed the first book in this series. Part 2, God willing, will focus on graduate school and will be published a couple of years after this initial 2024 publication. Until then, do not forget to scan the QR codes below for additional information or inquiries. Please share and purchase the book with whomever you think would benefit from its content. *Gracias.*

For links to each of the book versions (including the audio version with bonus content) please visit:

https://www.antonionutrition.com/

Alternatively, scan the QR code below:

To contact the author or request a speaking or business inquiry please visit:

https://www.antonionutrition.com/contact

Alternatively, scan the QR code below:

DEDICATION

To everyone who believed in me, even when I didn't believe in myself. May we pass on the practice of encouragement in a world full of hardship. To my loving, hard-working family that, to me, represents the American dream and the first-generation college dream. May we never forget where we came from, and those who paved the way for us. Lastly, to every student and person experiencing difficult times. You are not alone. Seek support, and you will find it. God bless you.

Sincerely,

Dr. Antonio Miranda

SUICIDE & CRISIS LIFELINE

Call or Text 988

NOTES

NOTES

NOTES

NOTES

NOTES

NOTES